AMERICA AT THE CROSSROADS

*For my granddaughter
Shaheen Alam Khan,
daughter of Nafees and Ali Khan,
with love*

Praise for the author's previous works

Akbar Ahmed is the 21st-century Muslim Alexis de Tocqueville. If one wants to know why the world and not just America needs America to be America…if one wants to appreciate how new useful knowledge can be created by what anthropologists call "participant observation research," if one wants practical suggestions for building a better world at home and abroad together; then read Journey into America: The Challenge of Islam by Akbar S. Ahmed and his intrepid team.

Dean Louis Goodman, American University, Washington, D.C.

[Akbar Ahmed] is the first one that has really tried to capture the rich texture of America. A brilliant idea…it's going to be very influential.

Ambassador J. Douglas Holladay

This is likely to be one of the most definitive works to date on the Muslim experience in the United States. It will have a catalytic affect and will in all likelihood stimulate a generation of scholars.

President Cornelius Kerwin, American University

Ahmed's media profile is now as high as that of any living cultural anthropologist. One does not have to agree with all his positions to recognize that, in the specific but crucial field of Islam and relations between Muslims and non-Muslims, his life's work has done much to advance the values of anthropology. His celebrity should be welcomed as a gift to the discipline.

Jonathan Benthall, former Director
Royal Anthropological Institute, in Anthropology Today

I have not read a work as insightful, erudite, and innovative on the challenge of American identity since Alexis de Tocqueville's Democracy in America. Akbar Ahmed sets a new paradigm in the ongoing debate on defining American identity.

Melody Fox, Berkley Center at Georgetown University

A timely and stimulating contribution to a critically important issue: The West's (and especially America's) relationship to Islam.

Zbigniew Brzezinski, former US National Security Advisor

Perhaps the most distinguished and versatile Muslim scholar in the English-speaking world today.

Dr. Lord Rowan Williams, former Archbishop of Canterbury and Master of Magdalene College, Cambridge

Akbar Ahmed is the greatest scholar of Islam in America and the world… nobody else stands so high…He is the Dara Shikoh of modern Islamic leaders.

Professor Stanley Wolpert, Author of Gandhi and Jinnah of Pakistan

Akbar Ahmed, the world's leading authority on contemporary Islam.

The BBC

AMERICA AT THE CROSSROADS

RACE, ISLAM, AND LEADERSHIP

AKBAR S. AHMED

First published in the UK by Beacon Books and Media Ltd
Earl Business Centre, Dowry Street, Oldham, OL8 2PF

First paperback edition published 2025

www.beaconbooks.net

Cataloging-in-Publication record for this book is available from the British
Library

ISBN 978-1-916955-61-5 Paperback
ISBN 978-1-916955-62-2 Hardback
ISBN 978-1-916955-63-9 eBook

Cover design: Raees Mahmood Khan
Cover image: veronika-bykovich-tOmHyJ3_NZY-unsplash

Contents

Preface

Since the publication of my *Journey into America: The Challenge of Islam* over a decade ago, much has changed in the United States, yet much remains the same. The book is based on a year's fieldwork with my team of young American scholars. Crisscrossing the length and breadth of the vast country, we focused on understanding the Muslim community in the context of American identity, visiting over seventy-five cities and one hundred mosques. The fieldwork resulted in a book published by Brookings Institution Press and a documentary film with the same title. Prompted by the tenth anniversary of the project in 2020 amid the devastating coronavirus epidemic, we began to assess the state of American society in the intervening years and where it would be headed in the future—particularly concerning the central focus of *Journey into America*, the relationship between Islam and America.[1]

Early in the documentary film, I expressed my reasons for launching the project: "For me, it was a journey of discovery. It was also my tribute to the land which had welcomed me and my family so

---

[1] I would like to express my warmest gratitude to Frankie Martin, great friend, scholar, colleague, and the senior researcher of the Journey into America project, who was central to the writing of this book and helped shape and form it.

warmly. It was a journey of discovery for my young team too. Of their own country. Of themselves. As we traveled, I was again struck by the beauty and grandeur of America. And the hospitality and generosity of its people. The new version of the film was shown early in 2020 at the American University in Washington, D.C., and at the Church of Jesus Christ of Latter-Day Saints Temple, the grand house of worship situated by the Washington, D.C. beltway. Our plan was to show the film at other venues, but the arrival of the malign virus stopped us in our tracks.

While commentators were talking with anxiety about a new kind of authoritarian America emerging, accelerating after the arrival of the coronavirus, it is also clear that the love of freedom, democracy, pluralism, and strong ideas of human compassion are still valued in the land. Examining the study anew, we were struck by its rich ethnography. There are detailed descriptions based on fieldwork of the major ethnic contours of society backed by finely drawn case studies. The core idea of *Journey into America* still holds the key to understanding American society and its relationship with its minorities like Muslims can best be explained by appreciating what I defined broadly as the three American identities, which have been in play since the English settlers first arrived in the New World: primordial identity, pluralist identity, and predator identity. Rarely in the social sciences do we note the geometrically neat and schematic matchup between theoretical models and actual communities on the ground and the durability and resilience of these models. At the risk of gross simplification, one by one, in sequence, we saw the three models in play since the fateful events that followed 9/11—under George W. Bush, the primordial identity, with Barack Hussein Obama (and his vice president, and later president, Joseph R. Biden), the pluralist identity, and with Donald J. Trump the predator identity. American commentators have themselves taken to calling Trump's policies "predatory," explaining how Trump wants to cast foreign leaders as "subjects" not "partners" (see, for example, David Frum on TV and in *The Atlantic*).[2]

These models are not watertight. Indeed, individuals may shift from one to another over time, as we note they seemed to do. But they give us a rough and ready image and idea of a certain distinct type of American society. The presidents thus become emblematic of a particular model of American identity. This method can help us make sense of American society since 9/11.

---

2 David Frum, "Marauding Nation," *The Atlantic*, December 4, 2024; "America's Lonely Future: David Frum on Trump's 'Predatory' Foreign Policy," *Amanpour and Company*, PBS, December 4, 2024: https://www.youtube.com/watch?v=nIeUigGZktk

Introduction Retrospective—
Journey into America Revisited

More than a decade has passed since the publication of *Journey into America: The Challenge of Islam,* a work that sought to explore the relationship between Islam and American identity. As we revisit the project in light of recent events, it is also a fitting moment to reflect on the impact the book has had—across the political spectrum and in public discourse. I was thrilled, for example, when it was awarded the prestigious American Book Award, and I was able to discuss it widely in the media, such as CNN, where it was declared a "terrific read" on *American Morning,* the BBC, and Fox News. *Fox and Friends* described it as "a wonderful book...so comprehensive" and I also appeared on the *O'Reilly Factor* several times and was featured on Laura Ingraham's radio show. I additionally appeared on *The Daily Show with Jon Stewart,* and his producer informed me that I was the first guest they had ever had to discuss Islam specifically. "It's a great study," Stewart told me on the program, "it completely drives home the incredible diversity of something that I think, in our eyes, we view as a monolith, and anything that lends that, obviously, is very helpful." Some reviewers, spotting the similarity in the foreign provenance of the authors and their love of America, compared our study to that of Alexis de Tocqueville's classic book on America: "This is a must read—a new de Tocqueville on America for the 21st century."[3] My team and I also spoke about the book at many universities and events across the US, and the accompanying film was shown widely both in the US and worldwide, screening, for example, at the Parliament of the World's Religions in Melbourne, Australia. Barbara J. Stephenson, the Deputy Chief of Mission at the US Embassy in London, while introducing a screening of *Journey into America* at the Embassy, said, "Professor Ahmed is—quite simply—one of the greatest scholars of Islam in the world today...for me, *Journey into America* makes the essential discovery: that you can be an American and a Muslim and it diminishes neither your national nor your religious identity."

The book also happened to be released at the time of the controversy over the so-called "Ground Zero Mosque," in which a Muslim group promoting interfaith dialogue announced plans to build a center near the site of the destroyed Twin Towers. Their aim was to reach out and explain Islam to American society, but the project inflamed passions in the US and unleashed Islamophobia in mainstream America as the opponents of the center were offered equal time in the media to make their case. There were outlandish fears that Muslims were seeking to impose "sharia law" on Americans. A series of crises developed, involving opposition to mosques in places like Murfreesboro, Tennessee, and I was able to discuss these episodes in the context of *Journey into America* on programs like *Anderson Cooper 360* on CNN. Thus, a study like this was beneficial to help explain Islam and America to Americans. *Journey into America* was also translated into Chinese and published in China.

A decade later, when my team and I went back to the Journey into America project, both the book and the film, we felt that it had

---

3 A. B. McCloud, "Ahmed, Akbar. Journey into America: The Challenge of Islam," *CHOICE: Current Reviews for Academic Libraries*, Vol. 48, No. 6, 2011, p. 1146.

held up well. It is not an outdated and irrelevant study but one of current importance and, with its rich ethnography, a significant tool for understanding contemporary America. The time is right to return to the earlier project and apply its lessons to what is occurring in the US today. This new work also incorporates ethnographic fieldwork conducted in the United States since the publication of *Journey into America*. Frankie Martin, as the senior researcher for both projects, had never lost faith in them and vigorously argued to return to the themes of *Journey into America* and push them forward. Strongly patriotic, he believed fellow Americans would benefit from such an exercise. "As I looked back at *Journey into America*," Frankie noted, "I appreciated again the mammoth scale of the project and the contribution it has made and will continue to make. While working on *Journey into America*, I discovered my own country, and the project continues to embody and reflect the hopes and challenges of the US. I am proud that more than a decade on, *Journey into America* is still making an impact and has much to teach us. It helps us understand who we are as Americans and where we are going. I am thrilled that the research will be preserved and expanded in the context of contemporary American society in this small book."

Journey into America proved to be part of a more extensive journey we were on—a journey to understand the relationship between the Muslim world and the West after 9/11. The study followed one that my team and I had conducted in the Muslim world, *Journey into Islam* (2007). It was succeeded by the study *The Thistle and the Drone* (2013), about the global impact of the "war on terror," and *Journey into Europe* (2018) which examined Islam in Europe and the place of Islam in European history, culture, and civilization.[4] These four

---

4 Akbar Ahmed, *Journey into Islam: The Crisis of Globalization* (Washington, D.C.: Brookings Institution Press, 2007); Akbar Ahmed, *The Thistle and the Drone: How America's War on Terror Became a Global War on Tribal Islam* (Washington, D.C.: Brookings Institution Press, 2013); Akbar Ahmed,

projects, all published by Brookings Institution Press, constitute a quartet of studies on the same topic from different perspectives. They are based on anthropology and ethnographic fieldwork and, taken together, provide a unique view of Western-Islamic relations that can aid us in the crucial task of promoting better understanding and relations between peoples. Our current study in preparation, *The Mingling of the Oceans: How Civilizations Can Live Together*, continues these themes in investigating the best ways to promote coexistence from our shared human history.

The strength and relevance of *Journey into America* remain not just due to the thorough examination of Muslims in America, their history, and the accompanying detailed ethnography but its exploration of American identity and how Muslims and other minorities relate to it. Indeed, heated disputes and debates over identity divide society. Issues of race, ethnicity, and religion remain at the heart of the polarized state that America finds itself in today. Indeed, the killing of George Floyd by Minneapolis police in May 2020, yet another in a sequence of unarmed African Americans killed by often white police officers, proved to be a flashpoint in a racial reckoning that marked the mainstream ascendency of the Black Lives Matter movement. The movement and the widespread protests that followed shook the nation to its core, leading to counterreactions and debates over such matters as "Diversity, Equity, and Inclusion" (DEI) programs and "critical race theory." Additionally, developments such as the coronavirus pandemic with its politicization of vaccines, masking, and social distancing, the contentious debates over immigration, and the Hamas October 7 attacks in Israel and Israel's retaliatory devastation of Gaza have all profoundly influenced American society and their effects will continue to reverberate.

Journey into Europe: Islam, Immigration, and Identity (Washington, D.C.: Brookings Institution Press, 2018).

The main question we had set out to explore when we started fieldwork, "What does it mean to be American?" which lay at the heart of the ethnography in our study, remains as pertinent as when we first approached the subject. This book, *America at the Crossroads*, thus serves as a companion to *Journey into America*. Our ethnography, in the meantime, has not aged but remains a valuable source of information about American society, culture, and history. It also helps us understand the US today: there is cause and effect at work here, and it sets the stage for the coming time.

Chapter 1 American Identity in a Global Crisis

When America emerged blinking and unsure from the long night of the coronavirus, it entered a new world with dangerous challenges. Russia had invaded Ukraine, and although its all-out assault had ground to a halt with the redoubtable courage and resilience of the Ukrainians, the danger of escalation with NATO remained high. Relations between the US and China were drifting towards confrontation. China's meteoric twenty-first century rise and economic growth had been accompanied by glaring human rights violations, for example, the over one million Uyghurs incarcerated in camps in Xinjiang. The country's policy of strict COVID lockdowns, which initially seemed to produce success in stemming viral spread, turned disastrous when it generated political unrest and was ultimately removed, allowing the virus to circulate rapidly. China's internal problems, however, did not deter an aggressive policy of what it called Taiwan "reunification," creating alarm in the region. Kevin Rudd, one of the world's most pre-eminent China experts, published *The Avoidable War* and warned that a conflict with China would be "catastrophic." Henry Kissinger, in a conversation with the historian Niall Ferguson, who had worked on Kissinger's biography, pointed to the dangers inherent in the US-China confrontation and the threat it posed to world peace. Kissinger said we were at the foothills of "Cold War II," while a year later, he updated this assessment: we had entered the mountain passes. Ferguson himself argued that we were already in Cold War II, which may well heat up at any moment, and called his book *Doom*. The US was in danger of falling into the trap of a war on two fronts with two major opponents—Russia and China. The two giants sitting on top of the world, the US and China, were wobbling. It was not encouraging for the rest of the world.

Despite the repeatedly stated intent of American policymakers to "pivot to Asia" in their strategic planning, however, the Muslim world remained front and center in Washington thanks to the continuing confrontation with Iran and the crisis in Gaza, which threatened to embroil the US and the world in a Third World War. The horrific Hamas attack on Israel on October 7, 2023, which killed 1,200 Israelis, the largest killing of Jews on a single day since the Holocaust in Europe, was followed by a ferocious assault on Gaza by the Israeli military, which killed 45,000 Palestinians by December 2024. US forces in the Middle East who were deployed to fight the so-called "Islamic State" or "ISIS"—itself an after-effect of the US 2003 invasion of Iraq—came under increasing attack by proxy forces of Iran. The US responded with counterstrikes on targets it said were affiliated with Iran. US troops were now again being killed in the Middle East, as in the case of the drone strike that killed three US troops in Jordan in January 2024. Amid increasing clashes between Israel and Hezbollah in Lebanon, Iran launched strikes on Pakistan, claiming it was attacking separatist targets in Baluchistan, and Pakistan responded by bombing Iran. The Houthis in Yemen attacked ships in the Red Sea in defense of the Palestinian cause in Gaza, and the US responded with a series of bombings against Houthi targets. The escalating tensions also saw Israel and Iran bomb each other's countries in unprecedented actions. Bashar al-Assad's regime in Syria collapsed entirely, and al-Assad fled to Russia. The fraught situation in the region seemed to be only getting worse and threatened to spiral out of control at any time.

The devastating impact of climate change was also visible on our television screens and newspaper headlines. The cyclones, hurricanes, typhoons, melting glaciers, flooded cities, droughts, and wildfires illustrated that climate change was a reality. Unless the world acted in unison to tackle or control carbon emissions, it would be too late, and planetary catastrophe would be inevitable. Even this was not enough to convince the world at Cop 27, the UN global climate summit at Sharm el-Sheikh in Egypt in November 2022, to limit the global temperature rise to 1.5 degrees Celsius. The realistic figure would be about 2.8 degrees, scientists calculated. They predicted disaster. In August 2023 in Hawaii, the deadliest wildfire in US history killed 100 people, and the previous month of July 2023 was declared the hottest month in 120,000 years.[5] Inflation was out of control, and food scarcity was recorded in the United States. Several nations were already facing severe famine. There were heartbreaking scenes on television of famished fathers in Afghanistan and Somalia describing with choking voices why they had to sell their small daughters.

The American response to climate change and, indeed, other crises, however, was once again complex and divided. Donald Trump and his supporters dismissed climate change, seeing it as a conspiracy of the "elite" and America's enemies. Trump claimed, "The concept of global warming was created by and for the Chinese in order to make U.S. manufacturing non-competitive."[6] When President Joe Biden's head climate change official, John Kerry, testified before the House Foreign Relations Committee in June 2023, the Republican members either denied that climate change was happening at all—Con-

---

5 Andrea Thompson, "July 2023 Is Hottest Month Ever Recorded on Earth," *Scientific American*, July 27, 2023.
6 Helier Cheung, "What does Trump actually believe on climate change?," *BBC News*, January 23, 2020.

gressman Scott Perry dismissed it as "a problem that doesn't exist"— or put the blame entirely on China. Climate change was, therefore, politicized, ensuring that the full urgency of the matter had not yet dawned on the American public.

In the meantime, the fortunes of the Muslims in America itself took an upturn. When Trump became US president in 2017, succeeding Barack Obama, his first order was to issue what came to be known as the "Muslim ban," banning entry of people from several Muslim-majority nations into the United States. Trump first called for this action in 2015 when, as a candidate, he demanded "a total and complete shutdown of Muslims entering the United States." Just a few years later, after Joe Biden was elected in 2020, the 2022 midterm elections saw Muslims winning at least 83 seats at the local, state, and federal levels. "I ran because I wanted to make sure that we had representation in the halls of power," declared Bangladeshi American Nabilah Islam, the first Muslim woman and the first South Asian woman to be elected to the Georgia State Senate.[7] Biden himself nominated the first Muslim US federal judge, Zahid Quraishi, the son of Pakistani immigrants, who was confirmed by the Senate in 2021, and Nusrat Jahan Choudhury, a Bangladeshi American civil rights lawyer, who after confirmation became the first Muslim woman federal judge. Clearly, Biden's America was not Trump's America.

Even though overdue and tentative, the Muslim emergence in mainstream American politics traced a remarkable trajectory of the community, which followed the footsteps of others, as discussed in *Journey into America*. Commentators noted the historic nature of Muslims becoming federal judges, for example, comparing them to the first Jewish federal judge, Jacob Trieber, who was nominated by President William McKinley and confirmed in 1900. Trieber immi-

---

7 Yusra Farzan, "Record number of Muslims elected in US midterms: 'We should lean into who we are,'" *The Guardian*, November 26, 2022.

grated to the US at the age of 13 from Prussia and broke the streak of white Christian male federal judges that had endured since 1789.[8]

Muslim triumph reflected as much on American society as it did on its own leadership. It is the relationship between America and the Muslim community that forms the subject of *Journey into America,* and this work expands on its ideas. These shifts in political representation within the Muslim community reflect broader tensions in American identity, which we will now explore in greater depth.

---

8 Jenna Greene, "As first Muslim American judge, Quraishi joins long line of trailblazers," *Reuters,* June 10, 2021.

Chapter 2 American Identity and the Post-9/11 Domestic Landscape

It is helpful to remind ourselves of the broad American identities in *Journey into America*, which were simplified for analysis and discussion purposes. Primordial identity goes back to the landing of the English settlers on the North American continent, best personified by the early settlement at Plymouth: It was unmistakably white in color, English in language and culture, and Protestant in faith. This identity provided the foundation for normative American identity for centuries. The other two identities emerged out of this primordial identity.

The American Founding Fathers would personify our second identity, which we called pluralist identity. They enshrined Enlightenment-era principles of religious freedom, civil rights and liberties, and democracy in the nation's founding documents. The Founding Fathers included the different religions of the world in their conception of being American, including Muslims, Jews, and members of the non-Abrahamic faiths. Concerning Islam, for example, Thomas Jefferson, George Washington, and Benjamin Franklin welcomed Muslims to the US. Franklin expressed his wish that the Grand Mufti of Istanbul preach Islam to Americans from a pulpit in Philadelphia.[9] John Adams named the Prophet of Islam, along with figures like Confucius, as among the world's great seekers of truth.[10] It is to be noted, however, that American pluralist identity predates the Founding Fathers to figures such as Roger Williams in New England and the founding of Plymouth. Williams, the founder of the State of Rhode Island, said that the government should allow the practice of all religions, including the "Turkish" (Islamic).[11]

The third identity, which I refer to as predator identity, is defined by the often brutal lengths to which Americans were prepared to go to protect the purity of their ethnic community rooted in primordial identity. Predator identity is characterized by a "zero tolerance" policy towards the "enemy" and perceived threats to the community; it is also marked by a lack of self-reflection and self-analysis which allows the enemy to be demonized and targeted for destruction. Predator identity took shape in the early days of white settlement and was focused initially on the Native Americans. At first, the white settlers attempted to convert the Native Americans to Christianity. When Native Americans began to convert, the white settlers shifted the argument to that of color. Even if the Native Americans became Christian, they argued, their color was still not white. The safety of the Native Americans could not be guaranteed, especially in the face of continued conflict as the white population pushed west and seized native land. Predator identity would also focus intently on other minorities, such as African Americans.

One of the Native Americans we met at the Plymouth historical site during fieldwork and quoted in *Journey into America,* a Cherokee playing a Wampanoag, captured this history in a single statistic: "Let me give you a shocking number. Five hundred years ago, we made

---

9 Walter Isaacson, *Benjamin Franklin: An American Life* (New York: Simon and Schuster, 2004), pp. 111–12.
10 John Adams, *Thoughts on Government*, Pamphlet, 1776.
11 Sarah Vowell, *The Wordy Shipmates* (New York: Penguin, 2008), p. 136.

up 100 percent of what is the United States today. Today we make up 1 percent of the entire population." Examining American history through this perspective, we note that these identities are constantly in flux and can dominate at different times for different reasons. The three identities provide us with *ceteris paribus,* an almost scientifically mechanical method that can predict coming events and how Americans will react to them with reasonable accuracy. It is important to reiterate that our three models are not watertight and, to complicate matters, individuals may be ardent supporters of one type at one stage of their careers and a different kind at another. Most models in the social sciences are notoriously unstable, short-lived, unpredictable in their consequences, baffling to those not of the discipline, and in the end, perhaps of little value. In our case, however, based on empirical evidence and with the proper caveats, we can stand by our models, as they have stood the test of time.

Revisiting the project, the models of the identities hold up remarkably well. There has been a lack of general movement between the three identities in the years since my book was published, which is perhaps a function of the heightened tension in American society following 9/11 and the sense of being under siege. There is a general fear in the public about being under threat from some vague amorphous enemy. That enemy is often seen as the Muslim projected in stereotypes as "the terrorist next door." In fact, the average killings of Americans by non-Muslim Americans are considerably many times higher in number than Americans killed by Muslims. Indeed, the young activists who captured the attention of the country in 2018 during the March For Our Lives highlighted the dangers of the epidemic of mass shootings. In the period of a single month between March and April 2021, the US experienced at least 50 mass shootings.[12] By the end of 2023, the US had experienced over 600 mass

---

12 Madeline Holcombe and Dakin Andone, "The US Has Reported At Least 50 Mass Shootings Since the Atlanta Spa Shootings," *CNN*, April 20, 2021.

shootings every year for the previous four years.[13] While the image of the Muslim terrorist still looms large in America, on average in the US every year, guns kill over 38,000 people and in addition cause almost 85,000 injuries.[14] The Anti-Defamation League reported that 73 percent of deaths caused by domestic extremists in the US between 2009 and 2018 were by far-right perpetrators.[15] Nonetheless, the pervasive sense of fear, threat, and paranoia ensures that the proponents of the three identities remain, by and large, in their same identities.

Primordial Identity

Let us examine in greater detail the status of the American identities. As noted above, the recent presidents who generally reflect each identity are a good way to enter the discussion. Despite the predatory predilections of many of President George W. Bush's officials, such as Dick Cheney, the man himself was inclined to be in the primordial category. Just six days after 9/11, Bush visited one of Washington, D.C.'s most prominent mosques, where he quoted from the Quran and declared, "Islam is peace." Bush was saying that one could be strong in one's identity as an American Christian, as he was while understanding that Islam was not represented by the terrorists and that America is a land of religious freedom.

I recognized this when I attended a special iftar dinner to break the fast during the month of Ramadan at the White House and was seated at Bush's table. He spoke of the Abrahamic faiths, in which he included Islam. He conveyed a confident and comfortable aura. I told him that I appreciated that he had mentioned Islam as part of the Abrahamic faiths but also warned that when people associated

---

13 See The Gun Violence Archive, https://www.gunviolencearchive.org/
14 "Gun Violence," American Public Health Association, https://www.apha.org/gun-violence
15 *Murder and Extremism in the United States in 2018* (New York: Anti-Defamation League, 2019), p. 16.

with him attacked Islam as a faith, it contradicted everything that the US stated it was trying to accomplish in the Muslim world in terms of "winning hearts and minds." I mentioned Reverend Jerry Falwell calling the Prophet of Islam a "terrorist" and how it hurt and enraged Muslims everywhere. To this, Bush responded almost to himself, muttering something like, "I should have slammed that guy when he said that stuff." A few days later, I read that Bush was categorically distancing himself from Americans fanning the flames of religious hatred. The next time I was invited back to the White House, I was greeted cheerily by Bush as I stood in the reception line, "Hey Doc, I've got your book. Thanks for finding time for me in your busy schedule."

Bush's rhetoric on immigrants often echoed that of President Ronald Reagan, who too reflected primordial identity, famously quoting and adapting Massachusetts Bay Colony Governor John Winthrop's "City on a Hill" sermon which, as discussed in *Journey into America*, asserted that America had been granted to Christians by God so that they could create an ideal community patterned on the teaching of the Bible. For Reagan, welcoming immigrants was part of this vision, and he celebrated immigrants in his final presidential speech as "one of the most important sources of America's greatness." Reagan, who granted amnesty to three million illegal immigrants, argued, "The United States and our neighbors, particularly our neighbor to the south, should have a better understanding and a better relationship than we've ever had…Rather than talking about putting up a fence, why don't we work out some recognition of our mutual problems, make it possible for them to come here legally with a work permit… and open the border both ways."[16] Bush's father, President George H. W. Bush, said that illegal immigrants should have full access to Amer-

---

16 "George H. W. Bush And Ronald Reagan Debate On Immigration In 1980," *Time*, YouTube.com, February 3, 2017: https://www.youtube.com/watch?v=YsmgPp_nlok

ican schools and all other services and lamented, "We have…made illegal some kinds of labor that I'd like to see legal…We're creating a whole society of really honorable, decent, family-loving people that are in violation of the law."[17] After leaving the presidency, George W. Bush spoke of the importance of immigration and, in 2021, published *Out of Many, One: Portraits of America's Immigrants,* in which his painting of a Muslim woman in a hijab features on the cover. That book, appropriately, begins with the former president quoting John Winthrop.

In our fieldwork for *Journey into America,* primordial identity was superbly represented and articulated by Joanne Herring, whom Julia Roberts played in the film *Charlie Wilson's War* (2007), which depicted her efforts to arm the Afghans against the Soviet Union in the 1980s. The charming and gregarious Herring, a proud Texan and Republican descended from George Washington, addressed the Conservative Public Action Conference (CPAC) and was photographed beaming surrounded by George H. W. Bush, George W. Bush, and Jeb Bush. Herring summed up primordial identity when we asked her about American Muslims: "You are a different group, you do value your traditions just as we Southerners do, we don't want to give our traditions up…We in our country choose how to worship, and that is why our country was founded, and we want them to have this ability to choose." She said with a hearty chuckle, addressing Muslims, "There are things that I would find it difficult to live with, but you wouldn't like a lot of the things I live with." Islam was a "lovely religion" that "teaches us wonderful things" she averred. She spoke of her memories staying in Muslim homes and even a "marvelous" time when Saudi princesses, the daughters of King Faisal, tried to convert her to Islam. While she was not going to convert, she said, "I respect this religion, and I love these ladies," so to humor them, she prayed with them. For Herring, it was all in good fun. She thus was indi-

---

17 Ibid.

cating that while she defined American identity in essentially white Christian terms—"We consider ourselves a Christian country," she stated—it was also open and gracious enough to include anyone as long as they respected the rights of the majority population.

Since we met her, Herring devoted time and energy to her organization, Marshall Plan Charities, which she founded and directed to aid Afghanistan, raising $450,000 in Houston for one village. The Afghan government then announced its intention to apply her model to other villages across the country.[18] "I got this wonderful letter from the village elder," she said in 2016, discussing the initial village she assisted, "You can't imagine how grateful they are, not to me but the United States. They want to paint the village red, white and blue."[19] After the US withdrew from Afghanistan and the Taliban took over in 2021, Herring said, "My heart is just breaking from what I see. All these people are weeping over Afghanistan, but they're not doing anything to help them…If you don't understand the country you're dealing with and trying to help, you hurt more than you help…It's like a physician treating a patient without examining him."[20] With her easy, authentic charm, self-assurance, and broad compassion, she was a perfect and endearing example of American primordial identity.

Pluralist Identity

The advent of 9/11 revived American predator identity. Looking back at our fieldwork for *Journey into America*, however, there was a sense among many Americans that its excesses, for example, the use of torture by the US government in the war on terror, were too

18 Mike Snyder, "Decades after 'Charlie Wilson's War,' Houston Socialite Joanne King Herring Still Making a Difference in Afghanistan," *The Houston Chronicle*, March 11, 2018.
19 Claudia Feldman, "For Joanne King Herring, the Ideas Keep Coming," *The Houston Chronicle*, August 1, 2016.
20 Amber Elliott, "Joanne King Herring's 'heart is just breaking' over Afghanistan," *The Houston Chronicle*, August 25, 2021.

great. Barack Obama's election as the first Black US president and the euphoria and jubilation among many that accompanied it seemed to indicate that the pendulum was now swinging back towards pluralist identity. Commentators, in fact, assumed that pluralist identity had won out in the race for history. There were many explanations, for example, that we were entering a "post-racial" America, and Obama was shown dressed as a Founding Father on magazine covers. The most popular musical of the era was *Hamilton* by the Puerto Rican composer and playwright Lin-Manuel Miranda, who was inspired by a biography of Alexander Hamilton to compose a rap about him that he performed for Obama in the White House several months into his term. He later revised this rap for the wildly popular Broadway show which revived the Founding Fathers for a new generation and demonstrated their relevance for contemporary pluralist identity.

Obama spoke of the inclusive nature of America in all its ethnic, racial, and religious varieties to domestic and global audiences in rhetoric that denoted the influence of Martin Luther King Jr. He and his wife Michelle were consistently ranked as the most popular man and woman in America. Obama vowed "change," especially with respect to the Bush administration and its war on terror policies, such as the use of torture and its invasion of Iraq. He spoke passionately about closing the prison at Guantanamo Bay, and he signed an executive order on his second day in office that it be closed within a year. He also oversaw an expansion of the rights of minorities like LGBTQ Americans, such as the institution of same-sex marriage, and was declared "the first gay president" by *Newsweek* on its cover.

Obama's vision for the Muslim world was encapsulated in his soaring 2009 Cairo speech, in which he spoke of Islam's "proud tradition of tolerance," citing "the history of Andalusia and Cordoba" and explained, "I saw it firsthand as a child in Indonesia, where devout Christians worshiped freely in an overwhelmingly Muslim country." He spoke of the contribution of American Muslims: "Since our founding, American Muslims have enriched the United States. They have fought in our wars, they have served in our government, they have stood for civil rights, they have started businesses, they have taught at our universities, they've excelled in our sports arenas, they've won Nobel Prizes, built our tallest building, and lit the Olympic Torch." Obama went on to challenge the idea of the "clash of civilizations," and quoting from Jewish, Christian, and Islamic holy texts, called on his audience to "reimagine the world, to remake this world...The people of the world can live together in peace. We know that is God's vision. Now, that must be our work here on Earth."

After Obama, it was assumed that pluralist identity would continue to grow along a trajectory. Yet I felt cautious then, and these reservations proved correct. Obama represented pluralist identity, but it was an identity already reeling after 9/11, and Americans remained sensitive to an all-pervasive sense of threat, particularly from the Muslim community. *Journey into America* analyzed the dangers of "homegrown terrorism" and violence among the Muslim population, and there were notable instances after its publication, such as the Boston Marathon bombing in 2013, the San Bernardino shooting in 2015, and the Orlando nightclub massacre in 2016, at the time the deadliest mass shooting in US history with 49 people killed, all of which put additional pressure on the Obama administration amidst criticism that it was not doing enough to keep America safe. The latter two cases were seen in the context of the rise, expansion, and gruesome and appalling violence displayed on video of ISIS in Iraq and Syria and a series of terrorist attacks in Europe, which Americans saw on their television screens. In the face of intense opposition to the idea, Obama did not close the prison at Guantanamo Bay, as he promised to do or wind down the war on terror, which expanded in various countries, including a marked increase in the use of weaponized drones in Muslim societies, as discussed in *The Thistle and the Drone*. The sputtering out of such bold initiatives as the Cairo speech, which raised hopes for a new relationship with the Muslim world, and un-fulfilled vows, such as the closure of the prison at Guantanamo Bay, showed a pusillanimity that characterized Obama's administrative approach. He also deported around three million people from the US, about a million more than George W. Bush, who himself had deported over a million more than President Bill Clinton.[21] Thus, while Obama did represent pluralist America, it was a kind of restrained vision as he was always aware and conscious of how visceral and deep the hatred for him was coming from the predator model. Obama was on the defensive from the relentless attacks on him and open disrespect shown to him, such as when a white US congressman screamed, "You lie!" at him during a nationally televised address before a joint session of Congress. His cautiousness in office did not end up placating his opponents, as Obama might have hoped, and had no discernible effect on their attacks on him. It was Obama himself and what he represented to them that they resisted. It was Obama's destiny to be the champion of American pluralism, seldom sure of who in the majority population was supporting him and who was undermining him. Obama's pluralist platform would be taken up first by Obama's Secretary of State, Hillary Clinton, who failed in her bid to succeed Obama as president, and then by Obama's vice president, Joe Biden, a few years after Obama left office, resulting in a clash with President Donald Trump for the direction of the country.

Predator Identity

When Trump emerged on the US political scene during Obama's presidency, he was a perfect counterpoint to Obama and provided a focal point of support for Obama's opponents. Indeed, Obama was built up as an exaggerated caricature, and all the supposedly nega-

---

21 Alfonso Chardy, "Record Number of Deportations Took Place on Obama's Watch," *Miami Herald*, December 25, 2016.

tive features that caused nightmares to Trump's supporters were highlighted. Obama was seen as a Muslim, a communist, a socialist, a Marxist, a foreigner who had been infiltrated into America to do damage to the country. The contradictions and irony of the jumble of images were ignored. These descriptions were routinely featured on TV screens with Obama's picture on Fox News. In short, he was the antithesis to everything that Trump and those who loved America stood for; Obama had to be invented even if he did not exist. He was a living breathing target that mobilized support for Trump. It created the idea that there but for the grace of God who sent Trump was a potential national disaster.

The liberal and left-wing media vigorously launched equally stereotypical caricatures of Trump as a Russian agent, morally and financially bankrupt, and an incompetent buffoon. It allowed Trump to dismiss these attacks as "fake news" and underline the corruption of the media, which he called the "enemy of the American people." It was gloomy and confusing and induced a hypnotic depression in millions of Americans, especially the young. Among foreigners it produced incredulity as they saw the US, the giant of yesteryear, woefully lacking in leadership, gravitas and even common sense.

The predator identity that was unleashed after 9/11 driven by leaders like Dick Cheney had opposed Obama immediately and the backlash gained rapid strength throughout his presidency. The political attacks on Obama melded seamlessly with Islamophobia as his opponents, in focusing their attacks on Obama as an outsider and a threat due to his supposedly Islamic connections and sympathies, reinforced the general sense that Muslims were dangerous and not fully American, causing great alarm in the Muslim community.

Trump was as unambiguous a promoter of predator identity as one could think of. He made Bush seem a saintly liberal pluralist by comparison. Trump repeatedly argued in favor of torture, killing the families of terrorist suspects, banning all Muslims from the

United States, and cast immigrants as threats, highlighting the cases of families who had loved ones killed by "illegal aliens." The power and dominance of Trump in the Republican party meant that many who opposed him and his vision for America, for example certain promoters of primordial identity, held back from criticizing him and either supported him or stayed silent, thus overlooking his transgressions concerning, for example, minorities and women.

In office, Trump drastically restricted refugee admissions (cutting the admission of Muslim refugees by 91 percent) and his cabinet secretaries like Ben Carson referred to Syrian refugees as "rabid dogs."[22] The effects of his travel bans were immediate at the beginning of Trump's presidency, with some 100,000 visas revoked the day that Trump signed his first executive order and chaos broke out at US airports which were mobbed by pluralist protestors.[23] As a deterrent to immigrants seeking to enter the US, Trump separated immigrant children from families, causing the children untold trauma; there were numerous reports of sexual assault while in US custody and the children lacking basic necessities like toothpaste[24] (also see the documentary *Separated* in which children are described as locked in "cages"). It is noteworthy in light of the discussion of predator identity in *Journey into America* that Attorney General Jeff Sessions' memo implementing child separation was entitled "Zero-Tolerance"—the designation the Trump administration used for the policy.[25] Trump

22 David J. Bier, "U.S. Approves Far Fewer Muslim Refugees, Immigrants, & Travelers," *CATO Institute*, April 23, 2018; Alana Wise and Erin McPike, "Republican Ben Carson Compares Syrian Refugees to 'Rabid Dogs,'" *Reuters*, November 15, 2015.
23 Justin Jouvenal, Rachel Weiner, and Ann E. Marimow, "Public Safety Justice Dept. Lawyer Says 100,000 Visas Revoked Under Travel Ban; State Dept. Says About 60,000," *The Washington Post*, February 3, 2017.
24 Matthew Haag, "Thousands of Immigrant Children Said They Were Sexually Abused in U.S. Detention Centers, Report Says," *The New York Times*, February 27, 2019.
25 "Review of the Department of Justice's Planning and Implementation

administration aides and officials also discussed "detaining migrants on military bases and flying them out of the country on military planes."[26]

Trump several times publicly yearned for European immigration while decrying immigration from those countries with non-white, low-income populations.[27] Trump was explicit after lawmakers discussed immigrants from African countries, Haiti, and El Salvador in a meeting with him in the Oval Office. He responded, "Why are we having all these people from shithole countries come here?" He then suggested that the US should instead bring people in from countries like Norway.[28]

Trump's administration tried to curtail both illegal and legal immigration and effectively reverse the landmark 1965 Immigration and Nationality Act which took shape under President John F. Kennedy and was signed by President Lyndon Johnson, opening up America beyond white Europeans to the rest of the world. I described Muslim immigrants who came after this time as "Kennedy's children" in *Journey into America*. The act was itself a reversal of the 1924 Immigration Act, which was shaped by advocates of the eugenics movement and instituted strict curbs on non-Northern European immigration, including effectively barring Jews, Italians, Africans, and Asians, among other groups from the US. When President Calvin Coolidge signed the law, he affirmed, "America must remain American." The law was

of Its Zero Tolerance Policy and Its Coordination with the Departments of Homeland Security and Health and Human Services," Department of Justice, Evaluation and Inspections Division, 21-028, January 2021: https://oig.justice.gov/sites/default/files/reports/21-028_0.pdf

26 Isaac Arnsdorf, Nick Miroff and Josh Dawsey, "Trump and allies plotting militarized mass deportations, detention camps," *The Washington Post*, February 21, 2024.

27 Nicholas Confessore, "For Whites Sensing Decline, Donald Trump Unleashes Words of Resistance," *The New York Times*, July 13, 2016.

28 Josh Dawsey, "Trump Derides Protections for Immigrants From 'Shithole' Countries," *The Washington Post*, January 12, 2018.

assailed by a series of US presidents including Dwight Eisenhower and Harry S. Truman, who spoke of its "absurdity" and "cruelty," but Jeff Sessions, Trump's attorney general, described it as "good for America."[29] Sessions criticized the 1965 immigration act as "a law that went far beyond what anybody realized," and his former aide and Trump's right hand man, senior advisor and speechwriter Stephen Miller, repeatedly praised the 1924 act and supported "the idea of a complete ban on immigration 'like Coolidge did,' an apparent reference to the 1924 law."[30] When Miller was asked at a White House press briefing if Trump's immigration policies violated the spirit of the Statue of Liberty and the famous Emma Lazarus poem referencing "huddled masses," Miller denied that the Statue of Liberty was a symbol of immigration at all, stating that the poem was "added later."[31]

In terms of Islam, when a man at one of Trump's campaign speeches said, "We have a problem in this country. It's called Muslims…When can we get rid of them?" Trump merely replied, "We're going to be looking at that and many other things."[32] Trump said he was open to keeping a database of American Muslims or making them carry special ID cards that listed their religion. He talked of shutting down American mosques because "bad things are happening."[33] He

29 Thomas Lee, "Trump Can Learn a Lot from FDR's Refugee Policy," *The Hill*, February 13, 2017; Emily Bazelon, "Department of Justification," *The New York Times Magazine*, February 28, 2017.
30 Ben Mathis-Lilley, "Jeff Sessions Once Said Restrictions on Jewish and Italian Immigration Were 'Good for America,'" *Slate*, September 5, 2017; Katie Rogers and Jason DeParle, "The White Nationalist Websites Cited by Stephen Miller," *The New York Times*, November 18, 2019.
31 "Trump aide dismisses Statue of Liberty 'huddled masses' poem," *CBS News*, August 3, 2017.
32 Theodore Schleifer, "Trump Doesn't Challenge Anti-Muslim Questioner at Event," *CNN*, September 18, 2015.
33 Nick Gass, "Trump: 'Absolutely No Choice' but to Close Mosques," *Politico*, November 18, 2015.

vowed, "We're going to have to do things we never did before," things "that we never thought would happen in this country in terms of information and learning about the enemy," and he claimed, "Islam hates us."[34]

Trump's nearly halting of the refugee program from Muslim countries contrasted with Muslim nations like Turkey and Pakistan, who took in millions of desperate refugees and immigrants. The victims of his Muslim ban were some of the poorest and most desperate people in the world, for example, those from Somalia and Yemen. Even those Iraqis who helped American soldiers and were therefore at risk from their own people were denied entry to the US in the first version of the ban, which was effectively a death warrant for them. Trump's pluralist opponents were left shaken by his effectiveness, while his supporters saw him as the guardian of their threatened way of life. But the greatest test of these identity conflicts would not play out only in Washington. It would unfold in the lives of ordinary Americans—including Muslims, Jews, and immigrants—across classrooms, airports, and neighborhoods. It is to those stories we now turn.

---

34 Jose A. DelReal, "Donald Trump Won't Rule Out Warrantless Searches, ID Cards for American Muslims," *The Washington Post,* November 19, 2015.

Chapter 3 Living Through the Identity Struggle

Trump's sentiments about Muslims were no secret, and on his election victory over Hillary Clinton in 2016, my alarmed student Mattison Johnston had tears in class. Worried about my fate as an immigrant, she soon issued a tweet which was reported to me by my office: "My sweet old Muslim professor, all he wants to do is to love everyone and help everyone." God bless America, I thought.

There was thus a contrast in the effectiveness of Obama and Trump's early initiatives. While immediately upon assuming the presidency, Obama ordered Guantanamo Bay closed and he failed due to the backlash to this policy, Trump immediately ordered the Muslim ban. Trump succeeded after watering it down by dropping countries like Iraq and adding the non-Muslim nations of North Korea and Venezuela, which allowed it to be upheld by the Supreme Court. The expectation was that more countries were planned. This allowed Trump's supporters to say he delivered for them.

Trump beat the drum of hyper-nationalism with his slogan of "Make America Great Again." His message resonated with millions of Americans. He set out to reject and foil most of Obama's initiatives: climate change efforts, deals with China and Iran, shoring up allies like those in NATO, his Affordable Care Act, which revamped health coverage, and concerns for immigrants, especially those who had entered the US without documents as children. Trump also reversed prior American policy in his seemingly constant praise of Russian President Vladimir Putin, and amidst a rising China and India and assertive Russia, oversaw a sidelining and ignoring of NATO and the fading of the "special relationship" with the UK. Trump's open clash with China on trade, enacted as part of his election promise, resulted in a trade war costing the world billions of dollars. The Trump administration's anti-China rhetoric further increased with the coronavirus pandemic, which originated in Wuhan, China, and dominated Trump's final year of his first term.

Internally, building on and enhancing America's post-9/11 rejuvenated predator identity, Trump described a myriad of foes and potential threats to the US that he alone was qualified to stop in their tracks and defeat. Inevitably, these forces were largely immigrants and minority groups, and there was an open antagonism towards immigrants and an explicit assertion of white supremacy, which then fed into support for Trump, who reinforced it. In his first speech as a presidential candidate, Trump launched his campaign with these comments on Mexicans: "When Mexico sends its people, they're not sending their best...They're bringing drugs. They're bringing crime. They're rapists. And some, I assume, are good people." Trump's oft-repeated desire for a "wall" on the US border with Mexico was a symbol, applying, in addition to Latinos, to groups like Muslims and Arabs, any group which seemed to be threatening to the US. Trump seamlessly blended these "threatening" groups, for example, stating that "Middle Easterners," despite no evidence, were part of "caravans" bound for the US border from Central America, which he described as an "invasion."[35]

---

35 David Agren, "Migrant Caravan Members Unfazed by Trump: 'He'll Change His Thinking,'" *The Guardian*, October 26, 2018.

Some eight months after assuming the presidency in 2017, Trump spoke about neo-Nazi protestors in Charlottesville, Virginia chanting "Jews will not replace us" and those protesting against them in the same breath, saying that both groups contained "very fine people." All this underlines the continuing importance of notions of American identity, chief among them race and color.

The impact of Trump's words and rhetoric coursed through American society, reaching minority children, for example, who often had to deal with students and even teachers taunting them with Trump's language. Fatuma Hussein, a 16-year-old Muslim high school student in Maine who was born in Kenya, for example, reported in 2019 that she "heard classmates jeering 'build the wall' or 'ban Muslims' as she walked through the hallway" while, also in Maine, a substitute high school teacher "referenced the president's wall and promised a Lebanese American student, 'You're getting kicked out of my country.'"[36]

The Cost of Visibility

According to the Southern Poverty Law Center, "surging" racist movements grew by 55 percent in the Trump era.[37] There were shocking acts of violence perpetrated by those with predator ideologies. One such gruesome act was the August 2019 massacre in El Paso, Texas, where a white supremacist killed over 20 people in the deadliest attack on Latinos in the modern history of the US. The killer praised the perpetrator of the 2019 New Zealand Christchurch

---

36 Mike Elsen-Rooney and Ashley Okwuosa, "Immigrant Students Learn Hard Lessons About Racism at a Historically White High School in Maine," *The Boston Globe*, August 14, 2019; Hannah Natanson, John Woodrow Cox, and Perry Stein, "Trump's Words, Bullied Kids, Scarred Schools," *The Washington Post*, February 13, 2020.
37 Jason Wilson, "White Nationalist Hate Groups Have Grown 55% in Trump Era, Report Finds," *The Guardian*, March 18, 2020.

massacre of over 50 Muslims, warned of a "Hispanic invasion," and argued that white Americans were being "replaced" by immigrants.[38]

As Islamophobia grew after 9/11, another religious hatred re-emerged, that of antisemitism; both forms of prejudice saw an identifiable increase in the Trump era. Trump made numerous statements that commentators identified as anti-Semitic despite the presence of several prominent Jews in his own government, such as his son-in-law Jared Kushner and his daughter Ivanka, a Jewish convert. While a candidate, Trump told an audience of Jewish Republicans, "Is there anyone in this room who doesn't negotiate deals? Probably more than any room I've ever spoken." "Stupidly, you want to give money," he said, but "You're not going to support me because I don't want your money."[39] He also "tweeted an image of Hillary Clinton's face atop a pile of cash next to the Star of David and the phrase, 'Most Corrupt Candidate Ever!'; and released an ad featuring the faces of powerful Jewish people with a voiceover about them being part of a 'global power structure' that has 'robbed our working class' and 'stripped our country of its wealth.'"[40] Then, during an address to the Israeli American Council in Florida as president, he said, "A lot of you are in the real estate business because I know you very well. You're brutal killers, not nice people at all." Yet now making an odd pitch for their support, he continued, "But you have to vote for me—you have no choice."[41]

Acts of antisemitism that shocked the nation included the October 2018 Pittsburgh Tree of Life Synagogue massacre, the deadliest attack on Jews in US history, with 11 people killed. The perpetrator

38 John Eligon, "The El Paso Screed, and the Racist Doctrine Behind It," *The New York Times*, August 7, 2019.
39 Zack Beauchamp, "Donald Trump's Speech to Republican Jews Was Filled with Anti-Semitic Stereotypes," *Vox*, December 3, 2015.
40 Bess Levin, "Trump Goes Full Anti-Semite in Room Full of Jewish People," *Vanity Fair*, December 9, 2019.
41 Ibid.

was a white supremacist, Robert Bowers, who blamed Jews for bringing "caravans" of immigrants or "invaders that kill our people" into the US in order to achieve what the killer called "the destruction of American society and culture."[42] Trump was constantly warning about the "caravans" during this period in the run-up to the midterm elections. Bowers went on online tirades against the Jewish refugee charity Hebrew Immigrant Aid Society and warned: "Open you Eyes! It's the filthy EVIL jews Bringing the Filthy EVIL Muslims into the Country!!"[43]

Antisemitism was prevalent on social media, with the ADL estimating that some 4.2 million anti-Semitic tweets were sent in English alone in a one-year period between 2017 and 2018.[44] The situation was such that in the spring of 2020, the editor at large of New York's *Jewish Week* asked, "Is it still safe to be a Jew in America?" writing that in his fifty years spent covering American Jewish affairs, "I never encountered such a level of palpable fear, anger, and vulnerability among American Jews as I do today."[45]

In the midst of the rise in antisemitism, I understood that Jews and Muslims needed to build understanding between their two communities, and in my own small way I continued my efforts to challenge both Islamophobia and antisemitism and other kinds of hatred; for example, through my series of public dialogues with Judea Pearl, the father of the murdered *Wall Street Journal* reporter Daniel Pearl, numerous talks at Jewish institutions and houses of worship, by working with such organizations as the Muslim-Jewish Advisory

---

42 Adam Serwer, "Trump's Caravan Hysteria Led to This," *The Atlantic*, October 28, 2018.

43 Masha Gessen, "Why the Tree of Life Shooter Was Fixated on the Hebrew Immigrant Aid Society," *The New Yorker*, October 27, 2018.

44 *Quantifying Hate: A Year of Anti-Semitism on Twitter* (New York: Anti-Defamation League, 2018).

45 Gary Rosenblatt, "Is It Still Safe to Be a Jew in America?" *The Atlantic*, March 15, 2020.

Council of Greater Washington, and serving as a charter member of the Anti-Defamation League's Interfaith Coalition on Mosques (ICOM), which was founded to protect mosques and challenge attacks on them. Along with the Episcopal Bishop of Washington D.C. and the Senior Rabbi of the Washington Hebrew Congregation, I formed the First Abraham Summit, and the three of us were active after 9/11. In early 2020, I also testified before the US Congress on antisemitism at a hearing held by the United States Commission on International Religious Freedom, delivering my talk entitled "'A Very Light Sleeper': The Scourge of Anti-Semitism."

Hate crimes against Muslims also reached their highest levels ever recorded in the Trump era.[46] There were frequent reports of mosques being attacked and fired on and Muslim men and women being threatened, assaulted, injured, and even killed. Even individuals simply believed to be Muslim or associated with Islam were targeted, as in the case of Sandeep Dhaliwal, the Sikh sheriff's deputy who was killed in Houston in 2019, or Srinivas Kuchibhotla of India, who was killed in Kansas in 2017 by a white man who screamed "get out of my country" and then bragged he had shot "Iranians."[47]

Alarming Islamophobic cases included that of Raheel Siddiqui, a 20-year-old Pakistani American Marine recruit, whose death in 2016 at the US Marines boot camp at Parris Island, South Carolina, was attributed to suicide, a claim challenged by his family. They sued the Marine Corps for $100 million for "negligence on multiple levels of command," citing severe physical and psychological abuse from drill sergeants as the motivating factor behind Siddiqui's death.[48]

46 Katayoun Kishi, "Assaults Against Muslims in U.S. Surpass 2001 Level," Pew Research Center, November 15, 2017.
47 Sangay K. Mishra, "An Indian Immigrant is Murdered in Kansas. It's Part of a Spike in Hate Crimes Against South Asians," *The Washington Post*, March 7, 2017.
48 Todd Spangler, "Family of Dead Muslim Recruit Sues Marines for $100 million," *Detroit Free Press*, October 14, 2017.

It is likely that Siddiqui faced the same type of physical and psychological abuse as Lance Corporal Ameer Bourmeche and Rekan Hawez. Bourmeche recounted during the court-martial trial of Joseph Felix, Siddiqui's drill sergeant, that Felix forced him to sit in an industrial-grade clothes dryer and renounce Islam, turning on the machine when Bourmeche refused to do so and only releasing him when he renounced his religion out of fear of further harm. Hawez, an Iraqi Kurd recruit, also faced similar threats from Felix and testified that Felix and another drill sergeant placed him in a dryer in a similar manner to Bourmeche. Felix was sentenced to ten years in prison; the allegations included vivid descriptions of physical and verbal abuse, occasionally under the influence of alcohol, at Parris Island. Numerous witnesses testified at his trial that they heard him repeatedly refer to the Muslim recruits as "terrorist" and "ISIS."[49]

Another heartbreaking death involves Nabra Hassanen, 17, of Reston, Virginia. A warm, lively, intelligent young woman who had just completed her sophomore year of high school, Nabra was one of four daughters from a close-knit Egyptian family. She regularly attended the mosque during Ramadan for midnight prayers. She and her friends were walking back to the All Dulles Area Muslim Society (ADAMS Center) mosque after eating at a nearby IHOP before the fast began in the early hours of June 18, 2017, when a 22-year-old man, Darwin Martinez-Torres, began to argue with them while driving by the mosque. Eventually, he drove his car onto the curb and began chasing Hassanen and her friends, finally reaching Hassanen (who had tripped over her abaya) and hitting her with a baseball bat before driving off with her. Nabra was then assaulted a second time, both physically and sexually, before dying as a result of her injuries. The campaign "Justice for Nabra" was formed, which was centered on bringing Torres to justice for his crimes. However, her father sadly

---

49 Rory Laverty, "Marine Drill Instructor Sentenced to 10 Years in Prison for Targeting Muslim Recruits," *The Washington Post,* November 10, 2017.

noted that clarity about the nature of his daughter's death would never bring her back to life.

Journey into America highlighted the negative impact of Islamophobia and discrimination on the Muslim population, particularly for young Muslims growing up in the US. Polling in 2020 found there to be no subsiding of this problem, with 51 percent of Muslim families reporting their children being bullied due to their religion at school. The same poll also found that 60 percent of American Muslims reported being subject to religious discrimination.[50] Further pressure was placed on the Muslim community over the issue of "sharia law," with conspiracy theories spreading that there was a plot to impose it on Americans. From 2010, the year the "Ground Zero Mosque" controversy erupted, to 2018, 43 states introduced over 200 anti-sharia bills, and 12 states banned "sharia."[51] A 2018 poll found that 42 percent of Americans and 71 percent of Republicans believed Islam was not compatible with American values.[52]

Flying While Muslim

Muslims also continued to be subjected to discrimination while flying, widely known as "flying while Muslim." There were numerous stories of Muslims being removed from flights, such as the case in 2016 when a young Muslim couple from Ohio was removed from a flight to the US from Paris, where they were vacationing, because a flight attendant overheard them use the word "Allah" and informed the pilot. "The woman was wearing a head scarf and using a phone,"

50 Dalia Mogahed and Erum Ikramullah, "American Muslim Poll 2020: Amid Pandemic and Protest," ISPU, October 1, 2020.
51 Swathi Shanmugasundaram, "Anti-Sharia Law Bills in the United States," Southern Poverty Law Center, February 05, 2018; Daniel Hummel, *Prejudice and Policymaking: Islamophobia in the United States and the Diffusion of Anti-Sharia Laws* (Lanham, MD: Lexington Books, 2021), pp. 10-11.
52 Victoria Bekiempis, "Republicans More Likely to View Muslim Americans Negatively, Study Finds," *The Guardian*, November 1, 2018.

she noted, "and the man was sweating."[53] A Pakistani military delegation visiting the US in 2010 was also removed from a flight from Washington, D.C. to Tampa, Florida, where the delegation was to hold meetings with US Central Command (CENTCOM), after "a tired member of the group was reported by a passenger who overheard him saying he hoped it would be his last flight."[54] "Flying while Muslim," noted the *Guardian,* "can range from extra questions from airport staff, to formal searches by police, to secondary security screenings and visa problems when visiting America. Sometimes, it feels like every Muslim has a tale to tell."[55]

This is certainly true in my case. I felt this high tension and mild humiliation on nearly every flight I took in the US. Every time I walked up to the airline counter and presented my ticket, a glazed look came over the face of the airline official. Discreetly, a phone was picked up. I was politely told to step aside and asked questions about my identity, what I was doing in that city, and why I was flying. Nothing identifying me seemed to matter except that my name was "Ahmed." I was assumed guilty and had to prove my innocence.

I recall one incident in particular because of how explicit it was at Reagan National Airport in Washington D.C. I was flying to a university in the Midwest to lecture on promoting better understanding between Muslims and Americans. I was already pre-checked and had my boarding pass. I stopped an airline official to ask about the security gate. She was a friendly African American woman. She smiled and said no problem, but then she looked down at my boarding pass. There was a flicker of recognition on her face as she saw my name, Ahmed. She said, "Oh no, you must come to the counter and check-

---

53 "Local Muslim couple removed from Delta flight: 'It was humiliating,'" *Cincinnati Enquirer,* August 5, 2016.
54 "Pakistan military taken off Washington airport plane," *BBC News,* September 1, 2010.
55 Homa Khaleeli, "The perils of 'flying while Muslim,'" *The Guardian,* August 8, 2016.

in there before proceeding to the security gate." I asked her why, as I had already obtained my boarding pass. What did she see that necessitated this scrutiny? "Is it because of my name?" I asked. She nodded in sympathy as she proceeded to type in my name, make discreet phone calls and start the procedure to check whether I was on some no-fly list. My age, profession, and status did not matter. My name was Ahmed, and that was sufficient to alert the system and merit scrutiny.

On such occasions, which perhaps involved overt forms of racism and religious prejudice, I was tempted to give a lecture on the meaning of the word Ahmed. The name meant "highly praised" and was an esoteric name for the Prophet of Islam. It was a derivative of Muhammad, the popular name of the Prophet. Muhammad, Mustafa, and Ahmed were the names of the Prophet whom Muslims blessed as "Mehboob-e-Khuda," or the beloved of God, and the Quran called a "mercy unto mankind." These names contain the most beautiful attributes and every time Muslims mentioned them, they added the words "peace and blessings be upon him." The name of the Prophet is also one of the most popular throughout the world; it is number one for boys in the UK, we were told during our fieldwork trips there, and it is especially popular in Muslim lands. My father's name was Muhammad Salahuddin Ahmed. Yet here in the United States, Ahmed could attract negative attention. In 2023, we at long last glimpsed the infamous "no-fly list" after leaked documents revealed the FBI-maintained database to contain around 1.5 million names, 98 percent of which were Muslim, according to an analysis by the Council on American-Islamic Relations (CAIR).[56]

---

56 Joseph Stepansky, "'Reeks of profiling': US 'no-fly' list appears to target Muslims," *Al Jazeera*, June 21, 2023.

The White House, Islam, and the "Clash of Civilizations"

In the environment of rising tension against the Muslim community during Trump's presidency, the president demonstrated his opinion of Muslims and their place in the US by nominating some of the most notorious Islamophobes to his administration, such as his first and third National Security Advisors, General Michael Flynn and John Bolton, CIA Director and then Secretary of State Mike Pompeo, Deputy Assistant to the President Sebastian Gorka, and Senior Advisor to the President Stephen Miller.[57] The most prominent of these was Steve Bannon, Trump's senior strategist and 2016 campaign manager, who was described as the president's "brain" and whose ideas continued to influence the administration long after his departure in August 2017.[58] Bannon headed the Breitbart News website, which he called his "killing machine," and was quoted making statements like "Darkness is good. Dick Cheney. Darth Vader. Satan. That's power."[59] Bannon had a worldview that was simplistic in the extreme and he personified what it means when we talk of "deep-fakes," "fake news," and "disinformation," all widely circulated and debated

---

57 See Mariam Khan, "Donald Trump National Security Adviser Mike Flynn Has Called Islam 'a Cancer,'" *ABC News*, November 18, 2016; Christopher Mathias, "John Bolton's Anti-Muslim Hate," *Huffington Post*, March 23, 2018; Bridge Initiative Team, "Factsheet: Stephen Miller," Bridge: A Georgetown University Initiative, November 30, 2018; Arsalan Iftikhar, "Mike Pompeo Said All Muslims are 'Potentially Complicit' in Terrorism. He's Unfit to be Secretary of State," *NBC News*, March 14, 2018; Bridge Initiative Team, "Factsheet: Sebastian Gorka," Bridge: A Georgetown University Initiative, December 5, 2018.
58 See Scott Shane, Matthew Rosenberg, and Eric Lipton, "Trump Pushes Dark View of Islam to Center of U.S. Policy-Making," *The New York Times*, February 1, 2017, and Steve Reilly and Brad Heath, "Steve Bannon's Own Words Show Sharp Break on Security Issues," *USA Today*, January 31, 2017.
59 Maxwell Tani, "'Darkness is good': Inflammatory Trump adviser Steven Bannon argues he, Darth Vader, and Satan are misunderstood," *Business Insider*, November 18, 2016.

terms in the anxiety following Trump's election. Bannon himself described his strategy for the media, which he viewed as the "opposition party," as, "Flood the zone with shit."[60] Bannon focused his attention soon after taking office on what he called the "deep state," meaning supposed anti-Trump, anti-American, and liberal forces ensconced in the federal government bureaucracy, and declared his goal to be the "deconstruction of the administrative state." He cited Lenin as an inspiration, declaring, "I am a Leninist...Lenin wanted to destroy the state, and that's my goal too. I want to bring everything crashing down and destroy all of today's establishment."[61] While Bannon was from a Catholic Irish family, he celebrated the legacy of the Protestant Scots-Irish in shaping the US, stating, "People say that the US is so divided. But here's the point, we are a revolutionary country. We broke off from the British, the biggest empire in the world, part of that is because of all those tough Scots/Irish that came over to the mid-Atlantic states with that born fighting attitude."[62]

Bannon embodied predator identity, focused as it is on the perceived threat from minority groups. These included Muslims, as Bannon described Bush's statement after 9/11 that "Islam is peace" as his "dumbest" comments as president and called "all" mosques "factories of hate." Breitbart articles placed African Americans in a specific category of "Black Crime"; for Latinos a representative Breitbart article read, "WARNING GRAPHIC: 9 Reasons to Fear Mexican Cartels More than ISIS" which alerted readers, "If They Want You, They Can Get You, Even In America...They Really Can Get You...Anywhere, Not Just On The Border...They Are In Your Neighborhood"; and concerning women and transgender people—"Does Feminism Make

60 Richard Stengel, "Domestic Disinformation Is a Greater Menace Than Foreign Disinformation," *Time*, June 26, 2020.
61 Ryan Lizza, "Steve Bannon Will Lead Trump's White House," *The New Yorker*, November 14, 2016.
62 Mandy Rhodes, "'We're the Ones on the Right Side of History': Interview with Steve Bannon," *Holyrood*, December 5, 2018.

Women Ugly?" and "Trannies Whine About Hilarious Bruce Jenner Billboard" were among Breitbart's stories.[63] While Dick Cheney was associated with Darth Vader during his time in office, Bannon's popular image was even darker—on *Saturday Night Live*, he was depicted as the Grim Reaper.

Bannon's core ideology, which has much in common with the European far-right with whom he was closely associated,[64] could be described best in his own words: the "Judeo-Christian West" is in deep crisis; it is threatened by an "expansionist Islam" and an "expansionist China." Consequently, we are heading for an apocalyptic "brutal and bloody conflict" that will take several decades to conclude. But the West is on "the right side of history" and will emerge victorious. Bannon explained that for Americans, this is the "fourth turning"—the first was the American Revolution, the second was the Civil War, and the third "the Great Depression and World War Two." In this brief and over-heated exposition, available on YouTube,[65] Bannon squeezes in a confusing jumble of incompatible ideological concepts, including Islamic jihadism, Marxism, and fascism, ideas that do not sit comfortably together.

In order to deal with this existentialist crisis, Bannon argued passionately for a simple and clear policy, one that Trump adopted hook, line, and sinker. The Bannon ideology rested on three broad ideas

---

63 Steve Reilly and Brad Heath, "Steve Bannon's Own Words Show Sharp Break on Security Issues," *USA Today*, January 31, 2017; Joseph Bernstein, "Here's How Breitbart And Milo Smuggled White Nationalism into the Mainstream," *Buzzfeed News*, October 5, 2017; Ildefonso Ortiz, "WARNING GRAPHIC: 9 Reasons to Fear Mexican Cartels More than ISIS," *Breitbart*, January 12, 2016; Milo, "Does Feminism Make Women Ugly?," *Breitbart*, July 26, 2015; Austin Ruse, "Trannies Whine About Hilarious Bruce Jenner Billboard," *Breitbart*, December 4, 2015.
64 See, for example, "Bannon plan for Europe-wide populist 'supergroup' sparks alarm," *BBC News*, July 23, 2018.
65 "This Historical Theory Explains Steve Bannon's Apocalyptic Worldview," *HuffPost Politics*, YouTube.com, February 8, 2017.

borrowed directly from Samuel Huntington's *The Clash of Civilizations* (1996) and *Who Are We? The Challenges to America's National Identity* (2004). The first recommends a zero-tolerance policy on immigration; the second, aggressive engagement with Islam and especially its "jihadi" elements; and the third, aggressive economic, political, and military confrontation with China with the aim to cripple, if not defeat the country. None of these points are original, and they are all at the core of Huntington's thesis. Bannon repeated them with the frenetic zeal of an undergrad discovering a self–help philosophy of life that would cure everything from erectile dysfunction to pimples. Trump, in turn, repeated them with the blind loyalty of an acolyte in the thrall of a charismatic, deranged guru, particularly after he saw results—by simplistically repeating the three points over and over again and adhering to the Bannonian formula, Trump was able to generate seemingly unlimited media attention, attract huge crowds, and ultimately defeat Hillary Clinton to achieve the ultimate American prize—the presidency. For Bannon, there was no hint of dialogue, humanity, or compassion in his worldview of brutal and bloody wars between civilizations. Affairs moved along on a straight line mechanically, deterministically, heading towards bloody apocalyptic conflict.

Bannon and Trump alike understood the appeal of and support for predator identity, particularly after 9/11, rooted as it is in race and religion—the primordial white Christian America. Bannon announced that Breitbart News was "the platform for the alt-right," the white nationalist movement that gained prominence during the 2016 presidential election—they were "Trump's shock troops," in the words of the BBC.[66] While the "alt-right" was commonly reported as a recent movement, often in the context of its online presence, tone,

---

66 Sarah Posner, "How Donald Trump's New Campaign Chief Created an Online Haven for White Nationalists," *Mother Jones*, August 22, 2016; Mike Wendling, "Trump's Shock Troops: Who Are the 'Alt-right'?," *BBC News*, August 26, 2016.

and tactics, in fact, it was often indistinguishable from the ideology of Pastor Thomas Robb, the Ku Klux Klan leader interviewed in *Journey into America*. Robb made news in 2016 when the KKK's official newspaper endorsed Trump with the headline "Make America Great Again," with Robb writing, "While Trump wants to make America great again, we have to ask ourselves, 'What made America great in the first place?'...America was founded as a White Christian Republic. And as a White Christian Republic, it became great."[67]

These experiences reveal the immense strain placed on America's pluralist fabric in the post-9/11 era. For Muslim Americans and other minority communities, the cost of this identity struggle has often been deeply personal—measured in fear, exclusion, and grief. Yet through these very trials, voices of resistance and solidarity have emerged to challenge the narratives of exclusion and hate. In the next chapter, we widen the lens to explore how the identity debates coursing through society have impacted another community at the heart of America's historical and ongoing reckoning: Black Americans.

---

67 Peter Holley, "KKK's Official Newspaper Supports Donald Trump for President," *The Washington Post*, November 2, 2016.

Chapter 4 Race and Identity

While the previous chapter focused on the lived experiences of Muslim Americans and the rise of Islamophobia in the post-9/11 period, the story of America's identity crisis is far from confined to any single community. Nowhere is the tension between pluralist and predator identity more historically entrenched and emotionally charged than in the Black American experience. From the legacy of slavery to the modern-day struggle against racism and police violence, Black Americans have long stood at the heart of the nation's moral and political contradictions. In this chapter, we turn to the voices, movements, and moments that have defined this ongoing reckoning—and consider how the fight for racial justice illuminates both the fractures and possibilities of American identity.

Inevitably, Trump's presidency saw increasing tension surrounding the issue of race and the place of Black Americans in the United States. Trump himself discussed African Americans in the context of urban crime and decay, declaring, "They are living in hell. You walk to the store for a loaf of bread, you get shot," and called cities with large Black populations like Baltimore "a disgusting, rat and rodent-infested mess."[68] Trump emphasized his self-described "tough" security-

---

[68] "Trump: 'African-Americans Are Living in Hell,'" *The Daily Beast*, October 26, 2016; Spencer Kimball, "Trump Calls Baltimore a 'Disgusting, Rat and

based "law and order" solutions to these problems while also touting economic growth. Trump additionally described Black athletes kneeling during the playing of the American national anthem, a practice begun by football player Colin Kaepernick as a protest against police killings of Black Americans, which he viewed as more respectful than sitting, as "sons of bitches."[69]

Tensions boiled over during the coronavirus pandemic following the killing of George Floyd by Minneapolis policeman Derek Chauvin in May 2020. Months of protests led by a reenergized and vigorous Black Lives Matter movement took place, and these protests resonated throughout the world. While Trump called Black Lives Matter a "symbol of hate," it was described as potentially the largest movement in American history—on a single day, June 6, 2020, "half a million people turned out in nearly 550 places across the United States."[70] Further motivating the protestors was the fact that the coronavirus was disproportionally affecting African Americans and other racial minorities—almost five times as many Black and Latino Americans were hospitalized with the virus than white Americans.[71]

The impact of these protests on the country was deep and profound and resulted in a discussion and debate about American identity and the scourge of racism going back to the institution of slavery. In the year after the protests broke out, some 170 monuments to Confederate leaders and soldiers were removed, and brands that fea-

---

Rodent Infested Mess' in Attack on Rep. Elijah Cummings," *CNBC*, July 27, 2019.
69 Jason Kurtz, "Trump's 'SOB' Remark Moves NFL Player to Kneel During Anthem," *CNN*, December 21, 2017.
70 Max Cohen, "Trump: Black Lives Matter is a 'Symbol of Hate,'" *Politico*, July 1, 2020; Larry Buchanan, Quoctrung Bui, and Jugal K. Patel, "Black Lives Matter May Be the Largest Movement in U.S. History," *The New York Times*, July 3, 2020.
71 William F. Marshall, "Coronavirus Infection by Race: What's Behind the Health Disparities?," Mayo Clinic, August 13, 2020.

tured stereotyped Black images, including Aunt Jemima, Uncle Ben's, and Cream of Wheat, announced they were altering their names, imaging, and packaging.[72] The heightened racial sensitivity also was applied to other groups like Native Americans, with Washington, D.C.'s professional football team changing its name from the "Redskins." Black Lives Matter was a strong, clear, and explicit rejection of predator identity, a local American response to an American problem. Its protests featured people of all backgrounds, giving pluralist identity wind in its sails heading into the 2020 presidential election.

These developments, of course, did not occur in a vacuum. When we were traveling during our fieldwork for *Journey into America*, we found simmering tension, particularly in America's cities, around race and relations with law enforcement, which continued to build over the coming decade. In 2012, George Zimmerman, a "neighborhood watch coordinator," a program overseen by local law enforcement, in a gated community in Sanford, Florida, shot dead Trayvon Martin, an unarmed Black teenager and 2014 saw flashpoints of conflict in Ferguson, Missouri and Staten Island, New York following the police killings of Michael Brown and Eric Garner. In Ferguson, protestors were met with armored police who looked like soldiers out of a combat zone with military equipment, shining a spotlight on the militarization of police in the post-9/11 war on terror era.[73] Black Lives Matter highlighted these cases and the tragically high number of others, bringing attention to an epidemic of unarmed Black men being killed by police who were often white. In 2015, Baltimore rioted following the death of Freddie Gray in police custody, and commentators pointed out a litany of factors, such as the fact that

---

72 "SPLC Reports over 160 Confederate Symbols Removed in 2020," Southern Poverty Law Center, February 23, 2021.
73 See Jessica Katzenstein, "The Wars Are Here: How the United States' Post-9/11 Wars Helped Militarize U.S. Police," Costs of War Project, Watson Institute, Brown University, September 16, 2020.

barely half of Baltimore's murders were solved and that the city had 16,000 vacant and abandoned homes.[74] Monica Villamizar of *Vice News* live-streamed interviews with Baltimore residents during the riots, and Black men she met made statements like "the police protect and serve society. We ain't a part of society. We're the enemies" and "They already look at us like we're animals."[75] One well-known commentator, Ta-Nehisi Coates, wrote, "We live in a country where the incarceration rate is 750 per 100,000. Our nearest competitor is allegedly undemocratic Russia at 400 or 500 per 100,000. China has roughly a billion more people than America; America incarcerates 800,000 more people than China," while another explained, "In March 2014 alone, police encounters in the United States resulted in 111 killings, twice as many as were killed by British police in the entire 20th century."[76]

During this period, there were also a series of burnings of Black churches and terrorist attacks against the community, such as the massacre of nine Black Americans at the Emanuel African Methodist Episcopal Church in Charleston, South Carolina, in 2015 by a young white supremacist, Dylann Roof. This was not an ordinary church but one of the oldest Black churches in the US, founded in 1816, and an important symbol of African American culture and identity. As Roof drew his weapon, he told his victims, "You are raping our women and taking over the country," rhetoric that he indicated in his manifesto was influenced by fears that whites were being demographically overtaken in Europe. He feared the same thing would happen

74 "Why Rioting Makes Things Worse," *The Economist*, May 2, 2015; Terrence McCoy, "Baltimore Has More Than 16,000 Vacant Houses. Why Can't the Homeless Move In?," *The Washington Post*, May 12, 2015.
75 "Raw Coverage from the Streets of Baltimore," *Vice News*, YouTube.com, Streamed live on April 27, 2015.
76 Ta-Nehisi Coates, "The Clock Didn't Start with the Riots," *The Atlantic*, April 30, 2015; Chandran Nair, "Foreign Lives Matter," *Foreign Policy*, April 30, 2015.

in the US.[77] Such tropes of "white genocide" and the "replacement" of whites by non-white minorities and immigrants were staples of white supremacist rhetoric online and the "alt-right." The sequence of police killings, as well as the church burnings and white supremacist acts of murder and terror such as Roof's, outraged much of the nation and led to the sense of exigency among Black Americans that rapid and sustained action was necessary.

In *Journey into America*, a passage from James Baldwin's *Notes of a Native Son* was quoted to illustrate the anguish and often rage among Black Americans in reference to the white community for how they were treated in American society. In an essay written in 1951, Baldwin asserts that there is "no Negro" in the US, "briefly or for long periods…who has not wanted to smash any white face he may encounter in a day, to violate, out of motives of the cruelest vengeance, their women, to break the bodies of all white people and bring them low, as low as that dust into which he himself has been and is being trampled; no Negro, finally, who has not had to make his own precarious adjustment to the 'nigger' who surrounds him and to the 'nigger' in himself." Some seven decades later, case after case of brutality and killings by white police were appearing with no end in sight—and the fact that these killings were being widely videotaped and circulated for the first time, including from police "bodycams," seemed to matter little. Into this atmosphere of building rage came the killing of George Floyd, the ultimate public execution. The result was an eruption that has still not dissipated.

Debates about US history and how to depict and analyze racism and slavery were invigorated by the George Floyd protests. They included promotion of, and resistance to, tools and methods includ-

---

77 Kathy Gilsinan, "Why Is Dylann Roof So Worried About Europe?," *The Atlantic*, June 24, 2015; Nick Corasaniti, Richard Pérez-Peña, and Lizette Alvarez, "Church Massacre Suspect Held as Charleston Grieves," *The New York Times*, June 18, 2015.

ing "critical race theory"—an approach originating in the field of legal scholarship and scholars like Derrick Bell, which focuses on the history and perpetuation of systems of "white hegemony" and the ways in which racism had become embedded in US laws and institutions—and *The New York Times* "1619 Project." The 1619 Project sought to frame, shift, and reorient the interpretation of US history from the time of the first African arrivals in Virginia who had been captured from a Portuguese slave ship and was spearheaded by the journalist Nikole Hannah-Jones. Hannah-Jones wrote passionately of the centrality of Black Americans to US history and the American story: "It is we who have been the perfecters of this democracy...despite being violently denied the freedom and justice promised to all, black Americans believed fervently in the American creed. Through centuries of black resistance and protest, we have helped the country live up to its founding ideals. And not only for ourselves—black rights struggles paved the way for every other rights struggle, including women's and gay rights, immigrant and disability rights. Without the idealistic, strenuous, and patriotic efforts of black Americans, our democracy today would most likely look very different—it might not be a democracy at all."[78]

When the 1619 Project was first launched, *The New York Times* announced that it was interpreting 1619 as "our true founding," thus overshadowing 1776 as the key year in American history. When controversy resulted about this, the language was altered to read that the *Times* aimed "to reframe the country's history by placing the consequences of slavery and the contributions of black Americans at the very center of our national narrative." The Trump administration, however, responded to the 1619 Project by initiating the "1776 Commission" to stress "patriotic education," with Trump calling the

---

78 Nikole Hannah-Jones, "Our Democracy's Founding Ideals Were False When They Were Written. Black Americans Have Fought to Make Them True," *The New York Times Magazine*, August 14, 2019.

teaching of issues like "systemic racism" to American children "a form of child abuse, in the truest sense…patriotic moms and dads are going to demand that their children are no longer fed hateful lies about this country."[79] Among those involved with the 1776 Commission was "Ex-officio" commission member Mike Pompeo, Trump's secretary of state, who assailed the 1619 Project in a speech on "human rights" as being an example of "Marxist ideology" and "a slander on our great people," leading to reactions of "shock and fury" from American diplomats.[80]

One by one, Trump's response to the issues and policies promoted by Black Lives Matter was to oppose, deny, and contradict, thus simultaneously adding to the urgency felt by many African Americans while echoing the views of Trump's supporters who cheered him on. When asked why Black Americans are being killed by police, Trump responded, "So are White people," and when asked whether "white privilege" exists, he said, "You really drank the Kool-Aid, didn't you?…No, I don't feel that at all."[81] Trump also ended the US government's diversity sensitivity training addressing such topics as white privilege and systemic racism, describing them as "divisive, anti-American propaganda."[82] As for "Defund the Police," a slogan adopted by Black Lives Matter activists and others that argued for diverting certain funds for police departments into under-resourced areas like social services and mental health programs, Trump asserted

---

79 Alana Wise, "Trump Announces 'Patriotic Education' Commission, A Largely Political Move," *NPR*, September 17, 2020.
80 Robbie Gramer, "Pompeo's Attack on '1619 Project' Draws Fire From His Own Diplomats," *Foreign Policy*, July 17, 2020.
81 Grace Segers, "Asked Why Black Americans are killed by Police, Trump Responds, 'So Are White People,'" *CBS News*, July 15, 2020; Eugene Scott, "'I Don't Feel That At All': Trump Scoffs At White Privilege In Woodward Book," *The Washington Post*, September 11, 2020.
82 Matthew S. Schwartz, "Trump Tells Agencies to End Trainings On 'White Privilege' and 'Critical Race Theory,'" *NPR*, September 5, 2020.

such calls were part of an "anti-cop crusade" and that "radical politicians are waging war on innocent Americans."[83]

Trump promoted the flag of the "Blue Lives Matter" movement, which was formed in response to Black Lives Matter and highlighted the deaths of police officers. Driving the movement were several high-profile shootings of police by Black men, including the 2014 killings of two New York police officers, which perpetrator Ismaaiyl Abdullah Brinsley said he conducted in revenge for the deaths of Michael Brown and Eric Garner, and the 2016 killing of 5 police officers, with 11 injured, at a Black Lives Matter protest by Micah Xavier Johnson, a former member of the US military who had served in Afghanistan. Johnson stated "he wanted to kill white people, especially white officers," in response to recent killings of Black people by police.[84] Trump highlighted such attacks on police in the context of his "law and order" focus and platform. These attacks and the killings by police alike further exacerbated the political, social, and racial divisions across the US.

While the Justice Department of the Obama administration investigated local police departments like Ferguson and exposed morally corrupt practices and racial bias,[85] Trump's reaction was the opposite, telling police to treat suspects roughly and not to worry about injuring them while making arrests: "When you see these thugs being thrown into the back of a paddy wagon…I said, 'Please don't be too nice'…the laws are so horrendously stacked against us, because for years and years, they've been made to protect the criminal. Totally made to protect the criminal. Not the officers. You do something

83 Katie Rogers, "Trump Continues Criticism of Movement to Defund the Police," *The New York Times*, July 13, 2020.

84 F. Brinley Bruton, Alexander Smith, Elizabeth Chuck, and Phil Helsel, "Dallas Police 'Ambush': 12 Officers Shot, 5 Killed During Protest," *NBC News*, July 7, 2016.

85 See "Investigation of the Ferguson Police Department," United States Department of Justice Civil Rights Division, March 4, 2015.

wrong, you're in more jeopardy than they are."[86] Trump also praised police actions and strategies such as "stop and frisk," in which any non-white person could be stopped and searched simply based on their appearance. Such an attitude ensured a "zero tolerance" response to crime firmly in keeping with predator identity.

Indeed, Trump was reflecting a certain attitude that developed among adherents of predator identity, particularly after 9/11, that seamlessly integrated attitudes towards the "external" Muslim enemy with the "internal" non-white "criminal." We can see this attitude in Dave Grossman, an ex-US Army Ranger and professor of psychology at West Point and "one of America's most popular police trainers."[87] An expert in what he calls "killology," Grossman has crossed over into popular culture. In Clint Eastwood's film *American Sniper* (2014), Grossman is quoted by the father of the main character, Chris Kyle, played by Bradley Cooper, as a life lesson to his children. Grossman presents his course, entitled "The Bulletproof Mind," to police across the US some 200 days a year. He tells his police audience: "Once you made the decision to take a human life, you're a transformed creature, you're a predator. What does a predator do? They kill. Only a killer can hunt a killer. Are you emotionally, spiritually, psychologically prepared to snuff out a human life in defense of innocent lives? If you can't make that decision, you need to find another job."[88]

The filmmaker Craig Atkinson, who attended one of Grossman's courses after being invited by the Ohio State Patrol Swat team in 2015, said, "He doesn't see the separation between Fallujah and Ferguson...And so he thinks of the police as the first line of defense to Al Qaeda, and there's no difference."[89] Grossman was clear on what

86 Meghan Keneally, "Trump to Police: 'Please Don't Be Too Nice' to Suspects," *ABC News*, July 28, 2017.
87 *Conditioned Response*, Field of Vision, documentary film directed and produced by Craig Atkinson and Laura Hartrick, 2017.
88 Ibid.
89 Kelly McLaughlin, "One of America's most popular police trainers is

he saw as the Muslim threat, and like Trump and the National Rifle Association responding to mass shooters, believed the solution was more armed "loyal Americans" capable of meeting the threat: "If you have Muslims in the workplace," Grossman said, "you have due cause to fear them. Offend their religion, offend them, and they and their family will come and kill you."—"There's one good answer, and that's armed, trained people everywhere."[90]

---

teaching officers how to kill," *Insider*, June 2, 2020.
90 Kira Lerner, "What the NRA's 'Professor of Killology' Thinks About The San Bernardino Shooting," *ThinkProgress*, December 4, 2015.

Chapter 5 Trump and Predator Identity

In the context of attitudes captured in ideas like "killology," I saw too well that Trump himself was not so much an aberration of American politics but a faithful representation of one part of it. This is confirmed by interviews from our fieldwork among white Americans in *Journey into America,* in which they expressed Trump's sentiments faithfully, if broadly. The difference was that now a president was saying these things. That was both his strength and his weakness: however outrageous his actions, those Americans who felt he represented them would continue to support him; those who were appalled by his actions found it difficult to accommodate to the predator model.

How should we understand and interpret Trump and his movement? Trump indeed pushed all the buttons of his base firmly anchored in predator and primordial identity. He became the champion of the whites in America who felt their country was being "taken" away from them, and in the context of anxiety about changing demographics—there were projections that in a few decades, the US would be "minority white."[91] *Journey into America* discussed and analyzed the alienated and angry white male opposing "elites," against demo-

91 William H. Frey, "The US Will Become 'Minority White' in 2045, Census Projects," The Brookings Institution, March 14, 2018.

graphic changes, perceiving insecurity and threat, and rooted in the history of Scots-Irish immigration and culture (see below). We met them in the field in places like West Virginia. The book quoted commentators like Michael Savage, who represented such a worldview: "If you keep pushing this country around, you'll find out that there's an ugly side to the white male that has been suppressed for probably 30 years right now, but it really has never gone away." Indeed, Savage was one of the first radio hosts to endorse Trump and authored the book *Trump's War: His Battle for America* (2017).

Upon his election as president, Trump attempted to place himself in the context of US presidential history, and the figure he seized on and associated himself with was not surprising—the Scots-Irish leader Andrew Jackson, the quintessential figure of American predator identity discussed in *Journey into America*. Jackson had explicitly challenged the pluralism of the Founding Fathers; for example, he refused to participate in the House of Representatives farewell tribute to George Washington as he felt that Washington was soft on Britain and too tolerant of Native Americans in the face of attacks on white settlers, and he castigated Jefferson as "too cowardly to resent foreign outrage upon the Republic."[92] Jackson also challenged the "elite," denouncing "the sordid and interested" and "moneyed aristocracy" operating through "secret operations" and asserting "the rich and powerful too often bend the acts of government to their selfish purposes."[93]

Trump tellingly revived Jackson, who he described as "a very tough person" with "a big heart,"[94] and celebrated Jackson's "history of tre-

---

92 Thomas M. Lessl, "Andrew Jackson (1767–1845)," in *U.S. Presidents as Orators: A Bio-Critical Sourcebook*, edited by Halford Ryan (Westport, CT: Greenwood Press, 1995), p. 68.

93 Jon Meacham, *American Lion: Andrew Jackson in the White House* (New York: Random House, 2008), pp. 122-123, 210.

94 Veronika Bondarenko, "Trump said Andrew Jackson could have prevented the Civil War—but the 7th president has an ugly history," *Insider*, May 1, 2017.

mendous success for the country."[95] Trump proudly placed Jackson's portrait in the Oval Office just days after his inauguration, ensuring Jackson's image would be, as Trump said, "right behind me, right, boom over my left shoulder."[96] Trump was thus constantly filmed and photographed next to the painting, giving it high visibility, and he visited Jackson's home in Tennessee, the Hermitage, as president two months after his inauguration. Trump laid a wreath at Jackson's tomb at the Hermitage to honor his 250th birthday and declared, "It was during the Revolution that Jackson first confronted and defied an arrogant elite. Does that sound familiar to you?"[97] Jackson's reputation as an "Indian killer" did not discourage Trump from identifying with him, and the comparison was actively encouraged by Steve Bannon.

White Grievance, "Deplorables," and the Scots-Irish Legacy

Trump's genius was to feed the fury emanating from segments of white America and the so-called "rednecks" and not placate their sense of grievance. He fed their anger and left their needs festering. He focused on their anger towards "elites," telling supporters in West Virginia, for example, "You are the elite. They're not the elite."[98] Trump checked all the boxes: Islamophobia, antisemitism, conspiracy theories (Trump appeared on the conspiracy promoter Alex Jones' internet show and hailed his "amazing" reputation), and the belief

---

95 Eli Rosenberg, "Andrew Jackson Was Called 'Indian Killer.' Trump Honored Navajos in Front of His Portrait," *The Washington Post,* November 28, 2017.
96 Ibid.; "President Trump Makes Remarks at the Hermitage," Trump White House Archived, YouTube.com, March 15, 2017.
97 Julie Hirschfeld Davis, "Trump Urges Supporters to Unite Behind G.O.P. Health Plan," *The New York Times,* March 15, 2017; "President Trump Makes Remarks at the Hermitage," Trump White House Archived, YouTube.com, March 15, 2017.
98 Michael Kruse, "Trump Reclaims the Word 'Elite' With Vengeful Pride," *Politico Magazine,* November/December 2018.

that Washington is corrupt, the media is fraudulent, or biased against "real" Americans, and elites are corrupt and disloyal to the USA. There was a clear "them" and "us" mentality. During the 2016 election, Hillary Clinton and Trump appeared to be on different planets. Even commentators could not believe Trump had a chance. However, they relied on normative American attitudes reflected in the media.

While running against Trump, Hillary Clinton, like Obama before her, used expressions seen as showing disdain for segments of white America we can broadly identify with the Scots-Irish—a marginalized population of Scots the British crown first settled in Northern Ireland before they journeyed to colonial America to settle the "frontier," for example, in Appalachia. During the 2008 campaign, Obama said of working-class voters in areas in which jobs had been lost, "They get bitter, they cling to guns or religion or antipathy to people who aren't like them or anti-immigrant sentiment or anti-trade sentiment as a way to explain their frustrations."[99] Clinton said that generally, half of Trump's supporters could be put "into what I call the basket of deplorables…The racist, sexist, homophobic, xenophobic, Islamophobic—you name it…Now, some of those folks are irredeemable, but thankfully, they are not America."[100] Trump's campaign and senior figures like Bannon then used the term deplorable as a term of pride, and Trump supporters began to identify as such. Their anger fueled support for Trump. His victory was almost guaranteed. As long as he had his base, he was secure. His intrinsic prejudices then burst out in office.

The so-called deplorables thus saw the elite as mocking and dismissing them, but they settled on one politician who was ready to champion them and to accept them as they were, warts and all.

99 Ed Pilkington, "Obama Angers Midwest Voters with Guns and Religion Remark," *The Guardian*, April 14, 2008.
100 Zeke J. Miller, "Hillary Clinton Says Half of Donald Trump's Supporters Are in 'Basket of Deplorables,'" *Time*, September 10, 2016.

Trump honed in on their fears and challenged the perceived Washington elite corruption, vowing to "drain the swamp." He confirmed their fears about Obama, for example, by vowing to expose his purportedly doubtful nationality and religion. Trump's "investigations" into Obama's birthplace, beginning in Obama's first term, confirmed among his followers their suspicions and beliefs that as a "Kenyan Muslim," Obama was a threat to the US and an illegal president. Trump also spoke in nostalgic terms to white America and against so-called political correctness on a wide range of issues, from toilets that used to flush with more water than more recent environmentally conscious models to lamenting that a South Korean movie, *Parasite*, won Best Picture at the Oscars, to vowing to "bring back" the ability to say "Merry Christmas." The deplorables had found their knight in shining armor in Trump, and nothing he said or did would shake their loyalty to him.

Wealth, Strength, and the Gospel of Winning

Trump's worldview was Darwinist in that he saw life as determined by the philosophy of the survival of the fittest. Indeed, *Journey into America* begins with a discussion of Darwinism associated with predator identity. Like a true Darwinian, Trump had praise and celebration for the strong and contempt for the weak who were seen as losers. While running for president, he openly mocked and mimicked a disabled reporter. His international relations policy seemed to be based on the notion of natural selection, and he was determined to make his nation "number one" in the world—his foreign policy doctrine was "America First." For the US to be up in his mind, other countries had to be down. He also prized strength and constantly spoke approvingly of himself or other figures doing things "strongly" and openly admired dictators like Kim Jong Un of North Korea, stating, for example, "He's the head of a country and I mean he is the strong head…Don't let anyone think anything different. He speaks and his people sit up at attention. I want my people to do the same."[101]

In statements made over the years, we see Trump's belief in the innateness of strength and other positive qualities as shaped through genetics, saying, "I'm a gene believer" and "I was born with the drive for success because I have a certain gene."[102] Trump said, taking aim at Jefferson's phrase, "All men are created equal. Well, it's not true. [Be] cause some are smart, some aren't." "Some people cannot genetically handle pressure," he explained, and expressed his belief that "winning is somewhat maybe innate...you have the winning gene." He linked his success to his ancestry, saying, "I'm proud to have that German blood." Trump's father was of German descent, while his mother was from Scotland.[103] Trump also reportedly told a black-tie gathering of senior British business and government leaders, including Prime Minister Theresa May, at Winston Churchill's Blenheim Palace in July 2018, "You've all got such good bloodlines in this room...You've all got such amazing DNA," and in September 2020 he told a nearly all-white crowd in Minnesota, an area with high Scandinavian settlement, "You have good genes. You know that, right? You have good genes. A lot of it is about the genes, isn't it, don't you believe? The racehorse theory. You think we're so different? You have good genes in Minnesota."[104]

---

101 Candice Norwood, "Trump: I Want 'My People' to 'Sit Up At Attention' Like in North Korea," *Politico*, June 15, 2018.
102 Caroline Mortimer, "Donald Trump Believes He Has Superior Genes, Biographer Claims," *The Independent*, September 30, 2016.
103 Marina Fang and J.M. Rieger, "This May Be the Most Horrible Thing That Donald Trump Believes," *Huffington Post*, September 28, 2016.
104 Shona Ghosh, "Donald Trump Complimented Guests on Their 'Great Bloodlines' in a Weird Speech to Top Business Leaders," *Business Insider*, October 11, 2018; John Haltiwanger, "Trump Told a Crowd of Nearly All White Supporters That They Have 'Good Genes,'" *Business Insider*, September 21, 2020.

Trump further embodied the value of material wealth and excess, which has roots in American society, as discussed in *Journey into America*, and the idea that whatever you have to do to become rich, famous, and be in the media and attract publicity is justified. Being wealthy was seen as a qualification for higher office, as Trump said in his speech announcing his candidacy, "I'm really rich." Wealth was perceived as indicating intelligence and a drive to succeed. Many Americans prizing hard work, business acumen, and entrepreneurship leading to material success—characteristics of Max Weber's "Protestant Work Ethic"—were attracted to Trump. He was already a media star, having hosted NBC's reality show *The Apprentice* for years, on which he appeared as a resolute and decisive CEO, and was himself his own brand embodying conspicuous wealth and luxury. For Trump, Obama's America was a wasteland, and he was the only one who could bring the nation back to prosperity and success, promising, "We will have so much winning if I get elected, you'll get bored of winning."[105]

Trump's vision can be clearly seen in his inaugural address, which Bannon, who co-wrote it, proudly described as "Jacksonian."[106] Trump portrayed American cities in ruin and collapse all around. It was a dystopian apocalyptic landscape. It echoed the lyrics of the song "Bad Moon Rising" by Creedence Clearwater Revival, emerging from the turmoil of the late 1960s and anger with the Vietnam War, which spoke of "rage and ruin" and warned of revenge where "one eye is taken for an eye." Trump discussed "American carnage" wracking the country and declared, "The forgotten men and women of our country will be forgotten no longer." He was thus reflecting the anger and grievance of his supporters back at them.

---

105 Julian Hattem, "Trumpmania Hits Capitol Hill," *The Hill*, September 9, 2015.
106 Robert Costa, "Bannon Calls Trump's Speech 'Jacksonian,'" *The Washington Post*, January 20, 2017.

Trump painted a bleak picture of America: "Mothers and children trapped in poverty in our inner cities; rusted-out factories scattered like tombstones across the landscape of our nation; an education system, flush with cash, but which leaves our young and beautiful students deprived of knowledge; and the crime and gangs and drugs that have stolen too many lives and robbed our country of so much unrealized potential." He vowed to "protect our borders from the ravages of other countries making our products, stealing our companies, and destroying our jobs." He also promised to "unite the civilized world against Radical Islamic Terrorism, which we will eradicate completely from the face of the Earth."

Trump at Home and Abroad

From the moment Trump was sworn in as president, he faced an onslaught as proponents of pluralist and also primordial identity immediately protested. Soon, there was non-stop news about Robert Mueller's investigation at the Justice Department into whether Trump's campaign colluded with Russia to win the presidency, followed by the investigation and first impeachment of Trump due to his blocking aid to Ukraine unless Ukrainian President Volodymyr Zelenskyy agreed to publicly investigate Joe Biden and his son Hunter's activities in the country. All the while, *The Washington Post* kept track of the number of false or misleading claims Trump made as president, counting over 30,000 by the end of his first term.

None of this was normal, and the result was that crises such as climate change were ignored or reversed. Under President Obama, measures to address climate change were not perfect but were heading in the right direction, and Obama also committed the US to the Iran nuclear agreement, which was working. Trump reversed both totally, withdrawing the US from the Paris Agreement concerning greenhouse gas emissions and scrapping the nuclear deal. Trump's natural instincts to "solve" problems like North Korea, Kashmir,

China, and Afghanistan were lost in the daily din and drama around his office, but he still resisted pressure to attack Iran save for his drone strike which killed the Iranian general Qasem Soleimani, nearly leading to a direct confrontation with Iran. While continuing the war on terror with an even more unrestrained policy, for example, towards drone strikes, Trump was erratic in his dealings with the Muslim world, at one moment verbally attacking Turkey and Pakistan and then the next welcoming their leaders, Recep Tayyip Erdoğan and Imran Khan, to the White House and praising them. In the Trump era, Muslims thus remained prominent as both villains and allies. Among Trump's closest allies was Saudi Arabia, which he visited early in his presidency. He spoke of 450 billion-dollar deals with the country, and the alliance was unshaken by the horrific murder of *The Washington Post* journalist Jamal Khashoggi by Saudi government agents in October 2018. Trump also oversaw a normalization of relations between several Muslim Gulf and North African states and Israel, but the deals left out the Palestinians, whose aid Trump cut off shortly after moving the US Embassy to Jerusalem and recognizing the city as Israel's capital, upending decades of US policy towards the region.

Among Trump's "hits" were: his expressed urge to "grab" women "by the pussy"; suggesting that hurricanes be nuked; stating that if Ivanka was not his daughter he would be dating her; diverting money from his charity for personal expenditure including buying a large painted portrait that made him look like a Marvel hero of the mutant category; refusing to condemn and disavow former KKK Grand Wizard David Duke's support for him; asserting that Republican senator and Vietnam prisoner of war John McCain was not a war hero because he was captured and "I like people who weren't captured"; paying off the porn star Stormy Daniels to keep quiet about an affair shortly before the election; pardoning US soldiers and contractors who committed war crimes against civilians in Afghanistan and Iraq;

suggesting sending American tourists infected with coronavirus to Guantanamo Bay; obsessing about his wall along the Mexican border and requiring his staff to acquire cost estimates of creating a moat on the border filled with snakes and alligators and proposing shooting immigrants who attempted to cross in the legs; banning transgender Americans from serving in the US military; telling four nonwhite US female members of Congress to "go back" to the countries they came from—all were American citizens and three were born in the US; and threatening to destroy countries like Iran, Turkey, and North Korea. It was no wonder there was a flood of books with titles like *Unhinged* from Trump's senior officials describing him as a demented and unstable man. The number of officials who resigned or were sacked from Trump's administration is striking. It is likewise striking the number of people indicted or convicted of crimes in Trump's orbit, including his personal lawyer, Michael Cohen, National Security Advisor Michael Flynn, advisor Roger Stone, campaign manager Paul Manafort, deputy campaign manager Rick Gates, advisor George Papadopoulos, and Steve Bannon, who was charged with defrauding Trump supporters who gave him money for the Mexican border wall. Trump ultimately pardoned Bannon along with Flynn, Papadopoulos, Stone, and Manafort. Those around the world were aware that the fate of the planet may depend on an unstable man—though Trump declared several times that he was a "stable genius." Yet through all of this, his base held.

Some 26 women also accused Trump of sexual assault and misconduct, and his defenses of innocence included stating that the women were too ugly to be assaulted, in two of the cases saying, "Look at her" and "Believe me, she would not be my first choice, that I can tell you," which likewise outraged his opponents and delighted his supporters.[107] There is also a relationship between Trump's election and the "Me Too"

---

107 "Trump Maligns Accuser: 'She Wouldn't Be My First Choice,'" *The Daily Beast*, October 14, 2016.

movement that erupted some nine months after he took office. "Me Too," first developed by the African American activist Tarana Burke a decade prior, was a direct challenge to societal misogyny. It led to women publicly stating their experiences with sexual assault. The movement had a global impact. It led to pillars of the American establishment being shaken as prominent male figures in numerous fields, including journalism, entertainment, business, and politics, lost their positions for engaging in patterns of sexual misconduct. Yet Trump, with his base behind him, weathered the storm.

Trump attained the presidency by appealing directly to the 30 to 40 percent of the population which remained his base and came to dominate the Republican Party. The devotion of his base explains his boast that he could shoot someone in the middle of 5th Avenue and not lose supporters. We saw that upon Trump's first impeachment at the end of 2019, he carried on as if nothing had happened, and his supporters likewise stayed with him after he was impeached a second time in 2021. His base was with him no matter what, and if Trump went from the political scene, those voters would follow another leader who spoke to them in the same language. That section of the country would remain loyal and cannot be ignored; that is the durability and strength of predator identity.

Trump became president at a time when the country was particularly polarized, and it only became more so in his tenure, with everything being seen through the lens of either Republicans or Democrats. The issue of whether or not to build the border wall, for example, was not discussed rationally but on an explicit partisan basis. Among the numerous political conventions Trump shattered which heightened the polarization were his personal and vicious attacks on Democrats, describing Speaker of the House Nancy Pelosi as a "lover" of the El Salvadoran gang MS-13 and stating that Democrats wanted MS-13 to "infest our country."[108] After Trump tweeted a doctored

---

108 Ramsey Touchberry, "Donald Trump Falsely Claims Democrats See MS-

image of Pelosi in a hijab and the Senate's most senior Democrat, Chuck Schumer, in a Muslim beard and turban, the White House press secretary accused Democrats of being "on the side of countries and leadership of countries who want to kill Americans" and that they are "taking the side of terrorists."[109]

Evangelical Support and the King Cyrus Analogy

The question of how evangelical Christians, a central base of Trump's support who championed Christian piety and values, could support him was frequently posed during his presidency. When confronted by the long list of lewd facts about Trump's life, his churchgoing followers simply dismissed the allegations and claimed that he was "sent" to them. Nothing would shake their devotion to him. However, it was interesting that they couched their arguments in religious terms. Their answer was given by Trump's conversion from a modern businessman with dozens of cases of fraud against him to a biblical figure deserving of admiration. The evangelists argued that while he may not be able to live up to the high ideals of a good Christian, he was like King Cyrus, who had freed the Jews from Babylon and was technically a heathen. So, Trump could do no wrong.[110] As Franklin Graham, one of Trump's most prominent evangelical supporters who compared the ten Republicans who voted to impeach Trump the second time to Judas, put it, "I never said he was the best example of the Christian faith. He defends the faith."[111] In other words, Trump

13 as 'Potential Voters' and Want Them to 'Infest Our Country,'" *Newsweek*, June 19, 2018.

109 Justin Baragona, "White House Claims Trump Boosted Fake Pelosi Hijab Image to Show Dems Take 'Side of Terrorists,'" *The Daily Beast*, January 13, 2020.

110 Adam Gabbatt, "'Unparalleled Privilege': Why White Evangelicals See Trump as Their Savior," *The Guardian*, January 11, 2020.

111 "Franklin Graham: Trump 'Defends the Faith,'" *Axios*, November 26, 2018; Jeffrey Martin, "Franklin Graham Compares 10 Republicans Who

was a warrior protecting the primordial identity of the US against its perceived foes—the very definition of predator identity.

Going into the 2020 elections, the result was a bitterly split country divided around 30 to 40 percent with mild fluctuation on most issues. It was also split along our three identities. As discussed above, none of the three were able to sweep the other two away or make dramatic headway. Yet, with Trump in the White House representing America abroad, the heartlessness of predator identity became commonly identified with America just as generosity, intelligence, and vision once did with presidents like Kennedy, Reagan, and Clinton. Now, Trump was seen as aggressively defining America.

Shortly before leaving his post as Secretary of State, Mike Pompeo summed up the attitude of Trump's administration in projecting America to the world. Discussing American identity, he declared it to be diametrically opposed to "multiculturalism" and being "woke," a term used to describe people who were concerned with racial and social justice issues, which was increasingly used by the American political right to define an opposing, anti-American, anti-white, or threatening force. For Pompeo, "multiculturalism" and "Woke-ism" are "not who America is" because they serve to "distort our glorious founding and what this country is all about. Our enemies stoke these divisions because they know they make us weaker. The United States of America is the greatest country in the history of civilization."[112]

These fractures in American society, sharpened by the rise of Donald Trump, were not fleeting disturbances but indicators of a deeper identity contest—one rooted in how Americans saw themselves, their nation, and each other. The events of Trump's first presidential term, which culminated in the storming of the Capitol, showed that predator identity had not only found a political champion, but had come

Voted to Impeach Trump to Betrayal of Christ," *Newsweek*, January 14, 2021.
112 Jason Lemon, "Mike Pompeo Opposes 'Multiculturalism,' Says it Distorts 'Glorious Founding' of U.S.," *Newsweek*, January 19, 2021.

to define America's image at home and abroad. Yet, even in the face of chaos, collapse, and violent extremism, another current was stirring—a pluralist resistance not entirely extinguished, steadily gathering momentum across communities, institutions, and individuals committed to the founding vision of a more inclusive America.

Chapter 6 Muslims and Pluralist Identity

Amid the turbulence of the Trump era, we note the emerging prominence of Muslims as pluralist identity asserted itself and primordial identity reached out to learn new lessons. Vilified through certain rhetoric and policy, Muslims were also propelled into the heart of the national conversation on identity, belonging, and constitutional values. The opposition to Muslims often sharpened their sense of purpose. As one of the luminaries of the American Muslim community, the convert to Islam Sheikh Hamza Yusuf, had told us during fieldwork for *Journey into America,* for Muslims "resistance is what makes you stronger. If you want to build your muscles you have to have resistance, but when there's no resistance there's nothing gained so I don't see this as necessarily a negative thing—it's a challenge."

In this chapter, we explore how Muslims, through public acts of courage, cultural expression, political engagement, and interfaith dialogue, asserted their place within American pluralism. Their journey reflects the broader struggle for dignity, representation, and recognition in a society caught between the three identities and the exclusion and embrace of minority groups.

Khizr Khan and the Constitution as Moral Compass

Take the example of Khizr Khan. During the 2016 Democratic National Convention, Khizr and his wife Ghazala stepped onto the stage, framed by a photograph of their son, Captain Humayun Khan, an officer who had given his life in Iraq to save his fellow soldiers in arms. With the national spotlight on him and representing a proud if mournful Gold Star family, Khizr Khan entered history. He spoke briefly, boldly, and clearly, embracing his Pakistani heritage as he pulled out a copy of the US Constitution and asked Trump if he had even read the founding document. Khan was arguing on the basis of the Constitution and the vision of the Founding Fathers that Trump's exclusion and disdain of the Muslim community was ultimately un-American. It was a moment that transfixed the convention audience—television images showed people with tears streaming down their faces—and the nation at large. The very idea that it was a Muslim man who challenged a flag-waving white American essentially celebrating white supremacy was in itself illustrative of the distance the Muslim community has traveled in a short while. While Muslims had made an impact in America before, like Muhammad Ali, this incident was emblematic of the larger process of change taking place. With a bow to Ali, it can be said that with one knockout blow, Khizr Khan rocked the dominant paradigm and social pyramid that had established Trump and people who thought like him at the top. Americans were suddenly looking at this minority group, which had been firmly placed at the bottom of the social pyramid, threatened with deportation, surveillance, and faith-based immigration bans, in a new light.

Trump himself predicably resorted to Islamophobic arguments, asserting that Khizr Khan had delivered the speech, not his wife, due to her status as a woman in Islam: "If you look at his wife, she was standing there, she had nothing to say, she probably—maybe she wasn't allowed to have anything to say, you tell me."[113] In fact, Ghazala Khan helped her husband write the speech but disclosed that she found it too difficult to speak about Humayun, as "I cannot even come in the room where his pictures are." As she wrote in *The Washington Post*, "without saying a thing, all the world, all America, felt my pain…My religion teaches me that all human beings are equal in God's eyes. Husband and wife are part of each other; you should love and respect each other so you can take care of the family…When Donald Trump is talking about Islam, he is ignorant. If he studied the real Islam and Koran, all the ideas he gets from terrorists would change."[114]

The tale of the Khan family may have marked a turning point in the process of "becoming American," similar to what had occurred in the past with other minorities such as African Americans, Catholics, and Jews, as discussed in *Journey into America*. It may well take a long time and require further struggle, sacrifice, and more active involvement from the Muslim community before measurable change is achieved, but the important point is that however slow and hesitating, the process had now begun.

During fieldwork for *Journey into America*, I visited Humayun's grave, which was shown to me by Colonel Jamie Martinez, commander of the Old Guard, George Washington's battalion, at Arlington National Cemetery. I realized in 2016 that I was now seeing the parents of that heroic soldier making a large impact on American society in standing up for American pluralist identity, which they and Humayun represented.

---

113 Maggie Haberman and Richard A. Oppel Jr., "Donald Trump Criticizes Muslim Family of Slain U.S. Soldier, Drawing Ire," *The New York Times*, July 30, 2016.
114 Ghazala Khan, "Ghazala Khan: Trump criticized my silence. He knows nothing about true sacrifice," *The Washington Post*, July 31, 2016.

Not long after the Democratic convention, I had the pleasure of hosting Khizr Khan at my home in Bethesda, in the suburbs of Washington, D.C., where family and friends waited to greet him. Overnight, he became a popular public speaker and frequently appeared in the American media. During our interview, he spoke of his vision for America and respect for figures like Jefferson, in whose backyard he lived in Charlottesville, Virginia. Khan said that his role models were the famous South Asian Muslim poet Allama Iqbal, Muhammad Ali Jinnah, the founder of Pakistan, Mahatma Gandhi, and "my history of Islam ends with the life of the Prophet." "All answers are there if you read the Prophet's life," he said, including the importance of "patience" and "warm-heartedness." Khan spoke of the "right to liberty" and "right to dignity." "That's what my Islam tells me," he said, which is also fundamentally American. With tears welling in his eyes, he said that to defend the US Constitution, you are defending these precepts. "This is your country," he said. "Protect it."

Hijab as Protest: The Women's March and Muslim Visibility

Following on the heels of the Khan family's emergence and Trump's inauguration in 2017 was the Women's March, a massive effort by adherents of pluralist identity voicing their opposition to the new Trump administration, which became the largest single-day protest in American history involving one out of every hundred Americans.[115] One of the most prevalent posters and signs carried by the marchers was a stylized image of Munira Ahmed, a Bangladeshi American from New York City who wore a red, white, and blue hijab, by Shepard Fairy, the artist behind the famous 2008 "HOPE" poster of Barack Obama. Ahmed was widely described as "the face of the

---

115 Matt Broomfield, "Women's March against Donald Trump is the largest day of protests in US history, say political scientists," *The Independent*, January 23, 2017.

Trump resistance,"[116] and in the words of CNN was "The woman whose face became a movement."[117] She affirmed of her experience marching, "It's beautiful to see so many women who are not Muslim, who are not South Asian like I am…everyone saw that as a relevant poster to hold."[118]

Other Muslim names now began appearing in the media, testifying to the strength of pluralist identity: there were the first two Muslim female congresswomen, Ilhan Omar, a refugee from Somalia, of Minnesota, and Rashida Tlaib, from a Palestinian American family, of Michigan. Both were elected in 2018, an election cycle that featured some 90 Muslims running for public office across the US, a substantial rise in visibility and political engagement for the community.[119] Omar and Talib followed into the halls of Congress Keith Ellison and André Carson, the two African American Muslim congressmen who were interviewed in *Journey into America*. In Virginia, several Muslims were elected to state office, including the state senator Ghazala Hashmi, the first Muslim woman elected to the state senate. In the 2020 elections, five states, Colorado, Delaware, Florida, Oklahoma, and Wisconsin, elected Muslims to their state legislatures for the first time. There were also stars in the mainstream media with an immigrant background: Hasan Minhaj, Aziz Ansari, Riz Ahmed, Mehdi Hasan, Ali Velshi, Ayman Mohyeldin, and Kumail Nanjiani—although several prominent Muslim news media hosts were mysteriously removed, especially after the Gaza war erupted, in what was widely perceived as an Islamophobic purge. Prominent women

---

116 Edward Helmore, "Munira Ahmed: the woman who became the face of the Trump resistance," *The Guardian*, January 23, 2017.
117 Kara Fox, "How a New Yorker became the face of anti-Trump protests," *CNN*, February 1, 2017.
118 Ibid.
119 Abigail Hauslohner, "The Blue Muslim Wave: American Muslims Launch Political Campaigns, Hope to Deliver 'Sweet Justice' to Trump," *The Washington Post*, April 15, 2018.

included Amna Nawaz on PBS, Samira Hussain on BBC television, and Sabrina Siddiqui, who wrote for the *Wall Street Journal* and appeared frequently in the news media. Muslim advocacy groups like ISNA and CAIR have also come of age and remain active on the national stage, promoting understanding and building bridges. Presidential candidates Hillary Clinton and Bernie Sanders additionally appointed South Asian American Muslims as key campaign staff members, Huma Abedin and Faiz Shakir respectively.

The African American Muslim community has continued to make a huge impact in the US in every field, documented in *Journey into America*. More recently, the debut album of the singer and songwriter SZA was among the best-reviewed of 2017—and named by *Rolling Stone* as one of the greatest albums of all time. Three years later Ibtihaj Muhammad, the fencer who competed for the US in the 2016 Summer Olympics in a hijab, became the first female American Muslim to win an Olympic medal. Barbie created a doll to honor her; it was the first to wear a hijab. The actor Mahershala Ali, who had become an Ahmadi as a young man, won Oscars in 2017 and 2019.

A Visit to the American Heartland in the Time of Trump

It would be safe to assume that Trump's advocacy of predator identity would influence other parts of the US, especially those regions where his support was high. What better way to find out than to visit the home state of Vice President Mike Pence, a staunch supporter of Trump and his philosophy? Yet my trip to Fort Wayne, Indiana, with Frankie in the fall of 2019 challenged that view and gave us several important points to consider in terms of this study.

Fort Wayne, with a population of 300,000, is known as the "City of Churches" with some 360. Still, about 7–8,000 Muslims live here. While there is said to be general Islamophobia in the state, there is also a community of white middle-class and middle-aged Americans led by Dr. L. Michael Spath, Director of the Indiana Center for Middle East Peace, who are consciously reaching out to make peace with the "other." Spath is a peace activist who leads groups of Americans on tours to the Middle East and promotes interfaith and intercultural dialogue.

Dr. Spath had invited me to address his Center and meet his colleagues. The first night he held a dinner for us in a private room at Chop's, a well-known Fort Wayne restaurant. It was attended by 32 guests, including four imams representing different parts of the Muslim community, as well as several top professionals, with at least two Pakistani doctors. Spath had thoughtfully arranged a prayer space for the Muslim guests with clean sheets neatly laid out on the floor pointing towards Mecca. At prayer time, one of the imams stood up and gave a beautiful call to prayer. The other guests looked on cordially while we prayed. Afterward, we had a question and answer session, and I was happy to talk about Islam and America. It was a moving gesture of respect for the Muslim community and a triumph of American pluralism.

The next day, it was time for the main event, which took place in a church hall. Michael was expecting a sizeable number of 40 to 50 people; in fact, we had an overflowing audience of about 150. All four imams in the region joined us, as did members of different ethnic communities, such as Afghans and Bosnians. I was very encouraged. The local Muslim community seemed united, confident, and showed signs of doing well; the women were vocal, visible, and confident. They told me they had no real problem living here, though one imam said that some non-Muslims were not happy with the idea of new mosques being built. Indeed, the only semi-hostile question for me came from a man who asked why mosques should be allowed in the US when there were no churches in Saudi Arabia, to which I responded that Saudi policy had its own way of interpreting religion, but Christians had lived by and large comfortably in most Muslim countries along with their churches; indeed I and my family, men and women, had been educated by priests and nuns in Pakistan. I also met a contingent of scholars attending the talk from Manchester University in Indiana who were studying ways to promote peace and had read my books.

Earlier in the day, we visited the Plymouth Congregational Church in Fort Wayne, and I spoke to the congregation and answered questions. This was the church where Michael's son Andrew, a professor and colleague at American University, was married. Frankie and I noted the name of the congregation and its reference to American identity. Throughout our visit, we found an atmosphere of comfortable social ease. What I experienced was far from the heated atmosphere and hatreds of Washington, D.C. It was the welcoming face of America, and it cheered us up.

At the end, summing up the visit, a beaming Michael told me that the Muslims "treated you like a rock star." He identified the aspects of my presentation that impressed him the most and which I suspect reflected his values. "You are a world-famous scholar, author, mystic, poet, and filmmaker who knows royals and celebrities. But what I find greatest is that you are student-centric." He spoke of the final scene in the *Journey into America* film, which we showed to the audience as part of my presentation. In it, I sit on the staircase of Jefferson's house, Monticello, with my young American research team. In this scene, I speak about the definition of America and reflect upon the statue of Jefferson at the University of Virginia, which contains a tablet held by an angel reading, "Religious freedom, 1786." The names of God in the different religions, including Allah, were listed on the tablet. To me, the statue perfectly encapsulates American pluralist identity. Michael told me to repeat this story at every gathering. "It sums up your attitudes," he said, "That is your dedication and vocation." After I returned home, he wrote, calling my visit "One of the great blessings in my life...During this time when in my world we focus on the incarnation of justice and peace and harmony, I just wanted to reach out with my gratitude for you and your lifetime of scholarship, building bridges, and goodwill. Blessings and peace, Akbar, to you and your family."

Our visit sparked the interest of local people who were part of Michael's community, like Victoria Gipson of Huntertown, Indiana, who was seated at Frankie's table during our first dinner in Fort Wayne. After talking with him and observing the night's program, she wrote to Frankie and me: "I so enjoyed our time together last evening. Frankie, myself, and others at our table had a stimulating discussion about the fact, unknown by many Americans, that Muslims have been a rich part of the religious fabric of our country since as early as the 1600s. I mentioned to you, Frankie, that I am somewhat of an aficionado of Thomas Jefferson, particularly his stance on religious freedom, and we discussed that among the many books in his library was a Quran. I was delighted when you, Dr. Ahmed, presented as part of your discussion last evening some of those same facts Frankie and I discussed at our dinner table about Locke, religious tolerance, and Jefferson's defense of Muslims, Hindoos, Jews, and others, defending their right to practice their faith and belief systems. Many Americans do not know their own country's history and, in particular, why Jefferson stood firm on his new country being secular and allowing for religious tolerance. Thank you for discussing this very important piece of US history...Frankie, you and I discovered that we had both spent time engaging with the Gullah/Geechee culture, and I was fascinated to learn of the material and cultural evidence of Islamic practices still to be found among those descendants of Georgia slaves. I wanted to learn and read more about this evidence of Muslims in colonial America. I was already aware that Muslims had served in the American Revolutionary War, but I did not know there has been preserved in this country evidence of colonial Muslim slaves writing, speaking, and reading Arabic as well as communicating to one another in Arabic, as a form of resistance to slavery. You both, with all of your research, are probably already aware of these facts, so you will have to forgive my enthusiasm in just now discovering this fascinating piece of Muslim American history. I look forward to this evening's presentation and want to thank you both for making the journey to Fort Wayne to share your knowledge and research with us."

There are a few lessons here for us. First, a great deal depends on leadership, whether at the community or national level. Michael, after 9/11, identified the Israeli-Palestinian conflict as the core problem alienating Americans from Muslims. He, therefore, began to visit the region every year with a group from his community. Overnight, these Americans from the Midwest saw their horizons broaden and had their eyes opened. They understood that all was not well in that region, and working for peace and mutual understanding was important. That is how the peace movement began, and the self-funded Center for Middle East Peace was opened.

The second lesson is that we have to live our own philosophy—as Gandhi said, to become the change we wish to see in the world. Michael, big-hearted, generous, jovial, and warm, is the embodiment of that vision. Lesson three is not to be misled by negative ideas, especially emanating from politics and the media. Real people are carrying on their lives and continuing to embody their values in local communities throughout the US. We saw this illustrated so well in this relatively small city. At the height of Trump, there was Fort Wayne.

Lesson four is to not underestimate the resilience of pluralism in America and the humanism in its society. Just as the triumph of predator identity was being hailed under Trump, challenges were being mounted by comedy hosts like Stephen Colbert, Trevor Noah, Jimmy Kimmel, and Seth Myers and politicians like Joe Biden, Bernie Sanders, and Pete Buttigieg, who emerged during the 2020 campaign season. They were a tribute to the vision of the Founding Fathers. The tussle between pluralist and predator identity reflects the complexity of American identity and testifies to its robust well-being. Finally, better understanding within societies can only come with better knowledge and information about "the other." That step can only be taken if there is sufficient humility in the seeker and persistent scholarship and engagement around him or her.

Chapter 7 American Crucible: COVID-19, the 2020 Election, and January 6

Upon our return from Indiana, the coronavirus hit the United States like the London blitz, causing a seismic cultural shock. The coronavirus advent in the United States had all the hallmarks of a science fiction black and white B movie of the 1950s, those with titles like *The Blob*, *It Came from Outer Space*, *The Thing*, and *The Day the Earth Stood Still*. The virus appeared from nowhere, was deadly, and its ambitions were global. The outcome of the encounter would determine the fate of human civilization, which hung in the balance. The virus did not differentiate between race, nationality, class, or religion. Black, brown, or white people were all vulnerable. UK Prime Minister Boris Johnson, Tom Hanks, Canadian Prime Minister Justin Trudeau's wife Sophie, senior Brazilian officials, and US congressmen all caught the virus early in the pandemic. Indeed, the world ground to a halt. In Saudi Arabia, the Kaaba was closed as pilgrimages were suspended, and Pope Francis canceled rituals at the Vatican. In the US, schools, malls, and businesses across the country were closed, and millions of workers feared for their jobs. This left the nation disorientated as it grappled with how to tackle the virus.

By the summer of 2020, nearly one million Americans had been infected with COVID-19, and almost 50,000 had died of the virus. The speed and deadliness of the coronavirus devastated the nation. Yet, despite the vast resources focused on discovering an antidote, no one in authority could say with absolute certainty how the virus came about and how it could be eliminated. When America first became aware of the threat from the coronavirus, it was dismissed in a characteristic manner through the lens of predator identity as a "foreign virus." President Trump referred to it repeatedly as "the Chinese virus." This was an arrogant view that echoed warnings of "the yellow peril" through much of US history. Soon, there were reports of attacks on Asians, especially those who looked "Chinese." Such attacks became common. The organization Stop AAPI Hate reported that over a year-long period beginning in March 2020, some 3,800 incidents of hate against Asian Americans were reported.[120]

At several early press conferences, Trump appeared confused in his response to the virus, reflecting his usual hastiness and dismissiveness as he praised his own greatness and that of the country—it was his natural temperament. His initial response was to say that everything was under control because he had instituted a travel ban and closed the borders; this proved sorely ineffective. The coronavirus then forced the leaders of America, including Trump, to climb down from their high horse and begin to understand that the world is intimately interconnected. It was widely reported that other nations like Taiwan, Japan, and Singapore were initially effective at containing the spread of the virus, while countries like the US lagged far behind.

The rapid spread of the coronavirus and the fear and panic apparent in the American public gave Trump an opportunity to turn the situation to his advantage. After an initial fumbling when he clearly had no idea—or experience—of how to deal with such a crisis, he ap-

---

120 Richard Fausset and Neil Vigdor, "8 People Killed in Atlanta-Area Massage Parlor Shootings," *The New York Times*, March 16, 2021.

peared resolute as he declared he was a "war-time president" and had put the country on a war footing. The choice of phrase was telling. He was moving naval ships about, ordering lockdowns, and mobilizing the state's vast resources. However, in his predator predilections, he cast himself not so much as a civilian orator rallying the nation like Winston Churchill but as a military general in the mold of his hero Andrew Jackson.

Using his quicksilver mnemonic talent to devastating effect, Trump had already labeled Mexicans as "rapists and criminals" and Muslims as "terrorists." The coronavirus gave Trump the perfect ethnic stereotype of the threatening foreigner as he repeated that it was "the China virus" and "kung flu." For his base, he was doing everything he had promised during his campaign: protecting Americans from aliens and illegal immigrants, attacking the elitist culture and "fake" media of the Washington D.C. swamp, and standing up to the Chinese. Yet again, in spite of every kind of calumny and slander they felt was hurled at him, Trump's base, by and large, continued to stand by their man.

Trump's "war" posture soon gave way to laxity in terms of virus prevention. He began promoting unproven remedies and halted his participation in regular White House coronavirus briefings after widespread mockery of his rumination that injecting disinfectant inside people's bodies might be an effective way to counter the virus. His focus turned to opening up the economy and developing a vaccine in record time.

From "Liberate Michigan" to the Capitol Riot

Trump's supporters' distrust of the "elite" seamlessly transferred to senior government health officials as they resisted officials' urges to receive vaccines and wear masks. They demanded an end to lockdowns, where many businesses and public gathering areas were closed or restricted. Against his senior medical experts, including Dr.

Anthony Fauci, head of the US National Institute of Allergy and Infectious Diseases at the National Institutes of Health, Trump unambiguously brushed away calls for Americans to take precautions such as wearing masks. In April 2020, after Trump tweeted, "LIBERATE MICHIGAN!" protestors with guns angry at Michigan governor Gretchen Whitmer's coronavirus measures forced their way into the state capitol building, a preview of the mob that burst into the US Capitol the following January. At least two of the Michigan protestors were among 14 people who were later charged in a plot to kidnap Whitmer and bomb the state capitol. And such were the threats to Dr. Fauci, who openly clashed with Trump on the government's coronavirus response efforts, that he had to have armed federal agents guarding him at all times.

Masks became a symbol of political identity, with a July 2020 poll finding that 86 percent of Democrats and those who lean Democratic stated that they wore masks every time they went out, while only 48 percent of Republicans and Republican-leaning Americans reported they wore masks every time they went out.[121] Trump was rarely seen in a mask, and even when he returned to the White House from Walter Reed National Military Medical Center after catching the virus himself and receiving experimental treatment, he removed his mask with great flourish before walking inside the building. Trump received the vaccine in private without an announcement, but nearly 30 percent of Republicans said they did not want the vaccine at all.[122]

Disinformation and conspiracy theories about the coronavirus spread widely. Trump often promoted them himself. In September 2020, Cornell University researchers found that the US president was the largest driver of misinformation about COVID-19. Medical ex-

---

121 Ben Kamisar and Melissa Holzberg, "Poll: Mask-wearing Divisions Remain Even as Coronavirus Cases Spike," *NBC News*, July 28, 2020.
122 Aallyah Wright, "Republican Men Are Vaccine-Hesitant, But There's Little Focus on Them," *Pew*, April 23, 2021.

perts at institutions like Johns Hopkins pointed to the prevalence of misinformation as the main reasons other countries were doing better than the US in fighting the pandemic.[123]

In contrast, as a presidential candidate, Joe Biden strongly focused on stopping virus transmission, supported scientifically informed public health policies, and was nearly always seen with a mask in public. After a few early stumbles, Biden surpassed the charismatic and visionary Bernie Sanders to win the Democratic nomination as the person to take on Trump. Biden swiftly nailed his pluralist colors to the mast. At the start of the month of Ramadan in April 2020, he sent a warm message to the Muslim community in which he acknowledged their contribution to America on different levels. He also made sure that he condemned the Muslim ban in strong terms: "I stand steadfastly with Muslim Americans against insidious and un-American actions like the Muslim Ban."[124] Biden had been inspired to run for the presidency after witnessing the white nationalist rally and violence in Charlottesville in 2017, which resulted in the death of a woman protesting against the white nationalists: "When those folks came out of the fields carrying those torches, chanting the anti-Semitic bile and their veins bulging, accompanied by the Ku Klux Klan, with such ugliness...I never thought I'd see something like that again in my life. That's when I decided."[125]

It was clear that without strong leadership, American pluralist identity would be on the ropes, and Biden proved his mettle, defeating Trump by winning over 80 million votes, the most in US history

123 Sheryl Gay Stolberg and Noah Weiland, "Study Finds 'Single Largest Driver' of Coronavirus Misinformation: Trump," *The New York Times*, September 30, 2020.
124 Joe Biden, "Statement by Vice President Joe Biden on Ramadan," *Medium*, April 23, 2020.
125 Graham Moomaw, "At Richmond Fundraiser, Biden Says He Wouldn't Be Running if it Weren't for Charlottesville," *Richmond Times-Dispatch*, August 27, 2019.

for a presidential election. Yet, further demonstrating the saliency of the identities, Trump received the second-highest number of votes ever, winning 11 million more votes than during his victory in 2016. However, on election night, Trump declared victory, and he never conceded or relinquished this claim. Many of his supporters thus believed shadowy forces had stolen the election from him.

One conspiracy narrative that Trump actively encouraged was the QAnon conspiracy theory, which held that Trump was fearlessly battling a network of satanic and cannibalistic pedophiles within the US government and power structures associated with the Democrats and other malign and secretive forces. QAnon was only the latest in a series of unfounded conspiracy theories in US history, often directly linked with antisemitism, asserting that the "liberal" and "international" elite was out to corrupt American society. One of these, said to be believed by some 12 million Americans, held that people in positions of power were actually reptiles, a theory originating in nineteenth-century ideas of alien species living amongst human societies disguised as people. Americans traced the theory to David Icke in England, who had been promoting his ideas that Queen Elizabeth was "a blood-drinking, shape-shifting alien."[126] During the 2016 presidential election, the "pizzagate" conspiracy theory, which maintained that Democratic Party officials were trafficking children for purposes of sexual abuse in locations such as the Comet Ping Pong pizzeria in Washington, D.C., where Satanic ritual abuse was practiced, circulated widely and led to QAnon.

The QAnon conspiracy held that "Q," a person purportedly at a high level of government who claimed inside knowledge of what was occurring, was issuing periodic statements, often clues or in code, telling followers what signs to look out for. They, in turn, scoured the public record for hidden meanings, for example in Trump's state-

---

126 Olga Oksman, "Conspiracy Craze: Why 12 Million Americans Believe Alien Lizards Rule Us," *The Guardian*, April 7, 2016.

ments. Trump publicly praised the movement, such as his August 2020 statement from the White House podium that QAnon followers were people who "love our country." When asked by a reporter what his response is to people who believe, "You are secretly saving the world from this Satanic cult of pedophiles and cannibals," Trump replied, "Well, I haven't heard that, but is that supposed to be a bad thing or a good thing? If I can help save the world from problems, I'm willing to do it; I'm willing to put myself out there. And we are actually, we're saving the world from a radical left philosophy that will destroy this country, and when this country is gone, the rest of the world would follow."[127]

Releases by Q and commentary by those in the movement that followed reassured followers that Trump was in control, even in the face of a demonstrated election loss, and that the country was in safe hands as he struck back at his enemies—including "globalist cabal" elites, Democrats, "the deep state," and Jews and Muslims. In short, with its prophecy-like religious rhetoric, which used terms like "Great Awakening," and paranoia about "elites" and non-whites, QAnon was reflecting important streams of primordial and predator identity.

January 6: The Siege of the Capitol

Following the announcement of Biden's election victory, Trump gave his blessing to a series of rallies where protestors gathered to condemn the election as rigged and proclaim Trump as the rightful winner. A considerable amount of tension built up, leading to January 6, 2021, when the US Congress would gather to officially certify the election results and Joe Biden's victory. Trump arranged a "Save America" rally in front of the White House on that day, in which he urged Congress, specifically Vice President Pence, to reverse the elec-

---

127 Zeke Miller and Jill Colvin, "WATCH: Trump says QAnon conspiracists 'love our country,'" *PBS Newshour*, August 19, 2020.

tion results, which Pence protested he could not do. Before Trump spoke at the rally, his lawyer and the former mayor of New York, Rudolph Giuliani, urged "trial by combat."[128] Trump told the crowd, "If you don't fight like hell, you're not going to have a country anymore" and used the word "fight" or "fighting" some twenty times. Trump used "peacefully" once while talking about the manner in which his supporters should march. He instructed them to "walk down to the Capitol" and "We're going to try and give them [Republicans] the kind of pride and boldness that they need to take back our country… you'll never take back our country with weakness. You have to show strength and you have to be strong." He focused intently, as he repeatedly had, on ballots sent in the mail—the preferred method for many concerned about the pandemic—as being fraudulent, stating, "using the pretext of the China virus and the scam of mail-in ballots, Democrats attempted the most brazen and outrageous election theft and there's never been anything like this." He vowed, "we will drain the Washington swamp and we will clean up the corruption in our nation's capital. We have done a big job on it, but you think it's easy. It's a dirty business. It's a dirty business. You have a lot of bad people out there."

Before long, the House and Senate sessions concerning the election had to be immediately adjourned as mobs broke through police barriers and entered the building, the very symbol of the American Constitution and government. Some carried the battle flag of the Southern Confederacy in the Civil War, reportedly the first time in history it had been flown inside the Capitol, and a scaffold and noose were erected outside the building. With millions of people watching live on television, the mob siege attack sent shockwaves through American society. Commentators abroad could not believe what they were seeing. Thousands of excitable and angry Americans attacked

128 "'Let's Have Trial by Combat' Over Election-Giuliani," *Reuters*, January 6, 2021.

the comparatively few policemen on duty, lives were lost, and the invaders deliberately expressed their intent to humiliate what they saw as a core symbol of America—they sat on the chairs of the most senior officials with their legs on the tables as a mark of disrespect, some defecated and urinated in the halls, and others tore up official documents and stole government property. Black Capitol police officers reported with anguish being subjected to racial abuse by the mob, with one exclaiming, "I got called a nigger 15 times today."[129] The mob had lists of targets as lawmakers were rushed to bunkers, with chants of "Hang Mike Pence!" ringing out. Nothing like this had happened since the assault two centuries before by an irate British army that attacked the Capitol during the War of 1812. The National Guard was eventually called in to restore order, but it took over 3 hours for them to respond.

The juxtaposition between how the Capitol is treated in American culture and the behavior of the mob was jarring and shocking for Americans. A visitor to the building feels the weight of history, they must even speak in muffled tones thanks to its hallowed status. Yet here were thousands of Americans, some in military-style gear and regalia and often displaying Christian symbols, attacking the building and the people in it in the name of "Saving America."[130] One of the rioters, a shirtless young man wearing a helmet with fierce horns who had painted his face in garish colors and carrying a spear with an American flag and an animal pelt, walked about on the Senate floor as if he had just landed on a Viking raid with his long boats docked nearby. A supporter of QAnon and a US Navy veteran, Jake Angeli was dubbed the "QAnon shaman" in the media and became one of the durable images of the attack. Standing behind Pence's recently

---

129 Emmanuel Felton, "Black Police Officers Describe the Racist Attacks They Faced as They Protected the Capitol," *Buzzfeed News*, January 9, 2021.
130 Elizabeth Dias and Ruth Graham, "How White Evangelical Christians Fused with Trump Extremism," *The New York Times*, January 11, 2021.

abandoned desk at the front of the Senate, Angeli led the assembled Trump supporters in a prayer to God, saying, "we will not allow the American way of the United States of America to go down...thank you for allowing us to get rid of the communists, the globalists and the traitors within our government. We love you, we thank you, in Christ's holy name, we pray."[131] Later, as he appeared in his police mugshot without his helmet and scrubbed clean, he looked a rather sad, bald, tired-looking young man, perhaps, one suspects, grappling with problems of erectile dysfunction. He had had his moment of glory in the sun.

Another QAnon follower, a US Air Force veteran named Ashli Babbitt, was shot dead by Capitol police as she tried to rush onto the floor of the House of Representatives. One man arrested at the Capitol, Lonnie Coffman, a US Army veteran, had driven from Alabama to Washington in a pickup truck with "an AR-15-style rifle, shotgun and handgun" as well as "a crossbow, stun gun and a cooler with 11 homemade Molotov cocktails" featuring homemade "napalm."[132] In his possession was a list of "bad guys," including Congressman André Carson, who he identified as "one of two Muslims in the House of Reps" (there were actually three). Carson, the chair of the House Subcommittee on Counterterrorism, Counterintelligence, and Counterproliferation, responded, "These were planned and organized measures to take my life, my colleagues' lives and try to destroy our government...Sadly, as a Black man and a Muslim fighting for equality, I have often been the target of death threats by domestic terrorists. For years, I have warned my colleagues about the serious threat to national security by white nationalist domestic terrorists.

---

131 Sebastian Milbank, "Shocking footage of Capitol riots," *The Tablet*, January 19, 2021.
132 Alexander Mallin and Mark Osborne, "D.C. Protester Arrested with 11 Molotov Cocktails, Several Guns Had List of 'Good Guys,' 'Bad Guys': DOJ," *ABC News*, January 12, 2021.

Seeing these seditionists rampage throughout the Capitol with their confederate flags, learning that many of the attackers had affiliations with law enforcement organizations, and then seeing the arsenals these attackers held, there should no longer be any doubt that this dangerous threat must be addressed as soon as possible. Everyone who supported these attacks must be identified and prosecuted to the fullest extent possible. No American should ever be targeted for violence or death because they are Black or Muslim, or because of their race or creed."[133]

The Aftermath of Insurrection

Immediately after the siege, Washington, D.C. was effectively locked down in advance of Biden's inauguration, with 25,000 troops deployed, more than were deployed at the time in Afghanistan, Syria, and Iraq combined. Soldiers and security forces set up checkpoints across the downtown area, and Capitol Hill was referred to as the "Green Zone" after the highly fortified center of government administration in Baghdad.[134] Americans were shaken by the sight of hundreds of troops camped inside the Capitol itself, reportedly the first time since the Civil War that this had occurred.

Respected voices in the country like General Stanley McChrystal, the former US and NATO commander in Afghanistan, warned in the days following the siege of the trials and dangers ahead for the country. McChrystal, who also served as the head of the US Joint Special Operations Command, related what the nation saw in Washington to Iraq and its al Qaeda affiliate, which developed into ISIS. In the case of al Qaeda in Iraq, McChrystal said, "a whole generation of angry Arab youth with very poor prospects followed a powerful

---

133 André Carson, "Rep. Carson Statement on Coffman Indictment," Press Release, January 12, 2021.
134 Rebecca Kheel, "Thousands of Troops Dig in for Inauguration," *The Hill*, January 17, 2021.

leader who promised to take them back in time to a better place, and he led them to embrace an ideology that justified their violence. This is now happening in America." McChrystal explained that Trump, with his narrative of an election victory, had created a new version of the "Lost Cause" narrative of the Confederacy after the Civil War—a just struggle foiled by treacherous elements: "President Trump has updated Lost Cause with his 'Stop the Steal' narrative that they lost because of a stolen election, and that is the only thing holding these people down and stopping them from assuming their rightful place in society…That gives them legitimacy to become even more radical. I think we're much further along in this radicalization process and facing a much deeper problem as a country than most Americans realize."[135]

For the United States' top military official, General Mark Milley, the Chairman of the Joint Chiefs of Staff, who served under Trump, the president's effort to steal the election was straight out of "The gospel of the Führer" and was "a Reichstag moment" in line with Adolf Hitler's seizure of power. Trump's MAGA supporters who flooded Washington, Milley said, were "brownshirts in the streets."[136] Former high-ranking military officials agreed, with General Barry McCaffrey describing Trump's MAGA movement as "a lawless cult" that posed "a major threat to the armed forces of the United States and our security." He warned, "what we are seeing is a parallel to the 1930s in Nazi Germany."[137]

Within a few months of the mobs overrunning the Capitol, the US government had over 450 ongoing criminal cases involving par-

---

135 James Kitfield, "Attack on Capitol Was the Beginning of an American Insurgency, Counterterrorism Experts Warn," *Yahoo News*, January 16, 2021.
136 Reis Thebault, "Joint Chiefs chairman feared potential 'Reichstag moment' aimed at keeping Trump in power," *The Washington Post*, July 14, 2021.
137 Lee Moran, "Retired 4-Star General Delivers Ominous Warning Over Trump's 'Lawless Cult,'" *Huff Post*, September 28, 2023.

ticipants, with the number steadily rising.[138] Some 140 Capitol police officers were injured defending the Capitol, and one died of a stroke after battling the crowd.[139] By the summer of 2021, four Capitol police officers had committed suicide after battling the attackers on January 6.[140] In July 2021, the House of Representatives formed a committee to investigate the January 6 attack led by the Democrat Bennie Thompson and the Republican Liz Cheney, the daughter of Dick Cheney. In December 2022, the House committee issued a criminal referral for President Trump to the Department of Justice for trying to overturn Biden's victory on four counts: "obstructing an official proceeding, conspiracy to defraud the government, making knowingly and willfully materially false statements to the federal government, and inciting or assisting an insurrection."[141]

The Trump era and January 6 distressed Americans and those around the world who looked to the US as a democratic model. The US was added to the annual list of "backsliding" democracies by the International IDEA thinktank, pointing to a "visible deterioration" which it said began in 2019, and "A historic turning point came in 2020-21 when former president Donald Trump questioned the legitimacy of the 2020 election results in the United States."[142] While the world watched the events of January 6 with horror, not long after, in fact almost exactly two years after, Brazilians staged a full-fledged attack on government offices, including the Congress and presiden-

---

138 Josh Gerstein, "Feds Move to Drop Charges for Capitol Riot Defendant," *Politico,* June 1, 2021.

139 Tom Jackman, "Police Union Says 140 Officers Injured in Capitol riot," *The Washington Post,* January 27, 2021.

140 Jan Wolfe, "Four officers who responded to U.S. Capitol attack have died by suicide," *Reuters,* August 2, 2021.

141 Dan Mangan and Christina Wilkie, "Jan. 6 committee sends DOJ historic criminal referral of Trump over Capitol riot," *CNBC,* December 19, 2022.

142 "US added to list of 'backsliding' democracies for the first time," *AFP,* November 22, 2021.

tial palace, while challenging the results of the presidential elections. It appeared to be inspired by what had transpired in the US.

Americans say, "It could never happen here," yet we saw it happening here. Historically, we have seen countries like France so easily slip from royalty, for example the government of Louis XIV, into anarchy and dictatorship. After the mob stormed the Bastille and initiated the French Revolution and the Reign of Terror, it was Napoleon who dispersed the mobs, ending the Revolution with cannons, what he famously called a "whiff of grapeshot," and became emperor. The storming of the Capitol in aid of Trump's cause was a reminder of how fragile the democratic American structure set up by the Founding Fathers, centered on the rule of law, actually is, especially when challenged by deep-rooted identities—the primordial and the predator.

It should also be noted that while there were pluralist figures like Roger Williams among the early colonists, primordial and predator identity dominated US history for nearly two centuries before the Founding Fathers and thus has a longer history than pluralist identity and the democratic system the Founding Fathers introduced. A large-scale poll published in July 2022 carried out by University of California scientists found that one out of every five adults in the US, "equivalent to about 50 million people, believe that political violence is justified at least in some circumstances."[143] The poll showed that "mistrust and alienation from democratic institutions have reached such a peak that substantial minorities of the American people now endorse violence as a means towards political ends."[144] In October 2022, David DePape of San Francisco, who had posted QAnon material online and invective against groups including "elites," Jews, and Muslims, tried to do just this in his attempted murder of Nancy Pe-

---

143 Ed Pilkington, "One in five US adults condone 'justified' political violence, mega-survey finds," *The Guardian*, July 20, 2022.
144 Ibid.

losi's husband Paul in their family home, which he had broken into looking for Nancy Pelosi.

These are ominous signs that people may be increasingly willing to resort to violence for the "protection" and "defense" of the "community" as they see it. In the aftermath of the Pelosi attack, the African American Congressman Jim Clyburn, a civil rights leader in the 1960s and senior ranking House Democrat, reflected these fears when he said that the US "is on track to repeat what happened in Germany" in the 1930s.[145]

---

145 Brad Dress, "Clyburn draws a parallel between US today and Germany before Nazis," *The Hill*, November 6, 2022.

Chapter 8 Pluralism in Power, Predator in the Wings

While President Joe Biden's critics accused him of being increasingly senile and infirm, he moved with the alacrity of a young man in a hurry in his first days as president. Within days of arriving at the Oval Office, he took a vigorous broom to the rubble left behind by Trump, and in short order, he removed the controversial Muslim ban, amended the immigration procedures, appointed John Kerry as the climate czar, and saw the rejoining of the US with the nations working to alleviate the impact of climate change in accordance with the Paris climate agreement. Then, inspired by the presidency of Franklin D. Roosevelt, Biden managed to pass a truly gigantic coronavirus relief bill of $1.9 trillion without a single Republican assisting him. Perhaps most momentous of all, he made available millions of vaccines and committed to injecting every American. With millions of Americans vaccinated, the nation was finally hoping it had controlled the pandemic. It was evident that pluralist America was vigorously attempting to return to the stage. In fact, Biden and his senior staff repeated the mantra "America is back." Biden's string of legislative victories included a $1 trillion bill to improve America's infrastructure in 2021 and the $745 billion Inflation Reduction Act in 2022, which contained energy provisions representing "the largest single step that Congress has ever taken to address climate change."[146]

The Three Identities in Biden's America

Yes, there was no denying that pluralist America had come roaring back. The election of Biden's vice president, Kamala Harris, marked the first time in history that a woman, and that too with an identity that included her Black Jamaican father and Indian mother, had reached the high office. Of course, predator identity did not let her get away without scorn being poured on the pronunciation of her first name—it was not an Anglo-derived name familiar to American primordial identity. In fact, Biden promised the "most diverse cabinet" of any president in US history, one that "looks like America." The cabinet was indeed historic in its pluralist nature: in addition to Vice President Harris, it featured the first female secretary of the treasury, Janet Yellen, the first Black secretary of defense, Lloyd Austin, the first openly gay cabinet secretary, Secretary of Transportation Pete Buttigieg, and the first Native American cabinet secretary, Secretary of the Interior Deb Haaland. Under Biden, some 3.5 million immigrants became US citizens, the highest number in any single presidential term in US history,[147] with the top source countries for the new Americans being Mexico, India, the Philippines, Cuba, the Dominican Republic, Vietnam, and China.[148]

---

146 Melissa Barbanell, "A Brief Summary of the Climate and Energy Provisions of the Inflation Reduction Act of 2022," World Resources Institute, October 28, 2022.
147 Muzaffar Chishti, Kathleen Bush-Joseph, Colleen Putzel-Kavanaugh, and Madeleine Greene, "Biden's Mixed Immigration Legacy: Border Challenges Overshadowed Modernization Advances," Migration Policy Institute, December 10, 2024: https://www.migrationpolicy.org/article/biden-immigration-legacy
148 "Demographics of Newly Naturalized Citizens," National Partnership for New Americans with data from the US Immigration Policy Center, University

Yet while pluralist America was strong and clear and back in power, its position remained wobbly as predator identity, rooted as it is in primordial identity, had never conceded its position. On the contrary, its leader, Trump, despite being banned from just about all major social media platforms for inciting violence, continued to use his foghorn to advocate for the politics he had instituted and had been rejected by Biden and the new administration. The fact remained that a large percentage of Americans remained loyal to President Trump. Recall that not one Republican Senator supported the initial coronavirus relief bill, and they had refused to convict Trump during his second impeachment for inciting the Capitol siege and riot. They likewise refused to vote to establish an independent commission to investigate the riot. In the face of logic, demands for unity in facing the national challenge of the pandemic, and the desire to right the wrongs of the past in the aftermath of the Capitol attack, the Republicans dug in their heels, and many still proclaimed that Biden had unfairly won the election. For anyone who might have thought that support for Trump had ebbed within the party post-presidency, the six-foot golden statue of Trump put on display at the Conservative Political Action Conference in Orlando, Florida, in February 2021 should have demonstrated the hold he continued to have. Among the conference's most popular attractions, it was a visual representation and metaphor of the fact that, despite beating the drum of their Judeo-Christian character, supporters were ignoring basic exhortations not to worship golden calves, or golden anything.

Trump's narrative that he had actually won the election contributed to Republican efforts to curtail voting access, with Republican lawmakers in 43 states proposing "at least 250 laws that would limit mail, early in-person and Election Day voting…potentially amounting to the most sweeping contraction of ballot access in the United

---

of California San Diego, May 14, 2024: https://partnershipfornewamericans.org/wp-content/uploads/2024/05/NAV_National-Stats-Final.pdf

States since the end of Reconstruction, when Southern states curtailed the voting rights of formerly enslaved Black men…The measures are likely to disproportionately affect those in cities and Black voters in particular, who overwhelmingly vote Democratic."[149] One such bill in Georgia implemented in March 2021, with provisions including making it a crime to give water or food to anyone waiting in line to vote, was described by Biden as "an atrocity" and "Jim Crow in the 21st Century."[150] QAnon also demonstrated its staying power in the country. A poll published in May 2021 found that 15 to 20 percent of Americans agreed with core tenets of QAnon, with 15 percent and nearly a quarter of Republicans believing, "The government, media, and financial worlds in the U.S. are controlled by a group of Satan-worshipping pedophiles who run a global child sex trafficking operation"; 15 percent, and nearly 30 percent of Republicans, believing, "Because things have gotten so far off track, true American patriots may have to resort to violence in order to save our country"; and 20 percent, and nearly 30 percent of Republicans, believing, "There is a storm coming soon that will sweep away the elites in power and restore the rightful leaders."[151] The poll further found that "just one in five Republicans fully rejected the premises of the QAnon conspiracy theory."[152] Robby Jones, the head of the Public Religion Research Institute, which co-sponsored the poll, noted the significance of the findings regarding the numbers of QAnon follow-

149 Amy Gardner, Kate Rabinowitz, and Harry Stevens, "How GOP-backed Voting Measures Could Create Hurdles for Tens of Millions of Voters," *The Washington Post,* March 11, 2021.

150 Maegan Vazquez and Kate Sullivan, "Biden Calls Georgia Law 'Jim Crow in the 21st Century' and Says Justice Department is 'Taking a Look,'" *CNN,* March 26, 2021.

151 PRRI Staff, "Understanding QAnon's Connection to American Politics, Religion, and Media Consumption," Public Religion Research Institute, May 27, 2021.

152 Giovanni Russonello, "QAnon Now as Popular in U.S. as Some Major Religions, Poll Suggests," *The New York Times,* May 27, 2021.

ers: "if it were a religion, it would be as big as all white evangelical Protestants, or all white mainline Protestants."[153] QAnon adherents also held conferences, such as the four-day "For God & Country Patriot Roundup" in Dallas, Texas, in May 2021, in which Trump's national security advisor and former head of US military intelligence, General Michael Flynn, who was filmed taking a QAnon oath and described Islam as "a cancer," called for a military coup in the US to remove Biden's government as had recently occurred in Myanmar, telling a cheering crowd, "it should happen here."[154] The previous month, Flynn had launched the nationwide "ReAwaken America" tour heavily influenced by QAnon and featuring "a swimming pool for a full-body immersive baptism in the name of the Lord" and "the blowing of the shofar—horns seen as spiritual weapons that herald the unleashing of God's power."[155] Trump continued to encourage QAnon, issuing dozens of Q-related posts on his "Truth Social" social media platform, including "an image of himself wearing a Q lapel pin overlaid with the words 'The Storm is Coming.'"[156]

New politicians emerged on the scene backed by Trump, such as Congresswoman Marjorie Taylor Greene of Georgia, who were featured heavily in the media. Greene had been a vocal supporter of QAnon, and her views included advancing a bizarre theory that California wildfires were caused by a laser from space launched by the Rothschilds, the Jewish banking family, and promoting a video

---

153 Ibid.
154 Stuti Mishra, "US Should Have Coup Like Myanmar, Former Trump Advisor Michael Flynn tells QAnon Conference in Texas," *The Independent*, May 31, 2021; Griffin Connolly, "Former Trump Aide Flynn Appears to Make Pledge to QAnon in July 4 Video," *The Independent*, July 5, 2020.
155 Ed Pilkington, "'He was chosen': the rightwing Christian roadshow spreading the gospel of Trump," *The Guardian*, November 6, 2022.
156 David Klepper and Ali Swenson, "Trump begins openly embracing and amplifying false fringe QAnon conspiracy theory," *PBS Newshour*, September 16, 2022.

asserting that "Zionist supremacists" along with "leftists" and "capitalists" formed an "unholy alliance" to flood Europe with immigrants, including Muslims believing in "sharia," to replace and commit "genocide" against whites, "breeding us out of existence in our own homelands."[157] Greene also warned of "an Islamic invasion into our government."[158] Other emerging pro-Trump Republicans like Congresswoman Lauren Boebert of Colorado made statements like, "How many AR-15s do you think Jesus would have had?…Well, he didn't have enough to keep his government from killing him."[159]

In April 2021, it was reported that Greene and other members of Congress were discussing forming an "America First Caucus" to continue and promote Trump's agenda. Its literature condemned the 1965 Immigration and Nationality Act, stated that immigration was putting America's "culture" and "identity" at risk, warned against "globalist institutions" and the "civilizational challenge" of China, and asserted: "America is a nation with a border, and a culture, strengthened by a common respect for uniquely Anglo-Saxon political traditions."[160] Shortly thereafter, President George W. Bush described the Republican Party as "nativist," an acknowledgment of how far attitudes against immigrants had swung. Bush pointed to the continuing strength of Trump—and predator identity—even after Trump left the presidency: "It's not exactly my vision…But, you know, I'm just an old guy they put out to pasture."[161]

157 Ben Sales, "Marjorie Taylor Greene Shared Antisemitic and Islamophobic Video," *The Jerusalem Post*, August 27, 2020.

158 Ally Mutnick and Melanie Zanona, "House Republican Leaders Condemn GOP Candidate Who Made Racist Videos," *Politico*, June 17, 2020.

159 Maya Yang, "Boebert tells Republican dinner guests they're part of 'second coming of Jesus,'" *The Guardian*, October 20, 2022.

160 Haley Talbot and Sahil Kapur, "Hard-right Republicans Forming New Caucus to Protect 'Anglo-Saxon Political Traditions,'" *NBC News*, April 16, 2021.

161 Quint Forgey, "Bush: Today's GOP is 'Isolationist' and 'Nativist,'" *Politico*, April 20, 2021.

Attacks on Asian Americans, which had risen markedly when the pandemic broke out, continued, with a 21-year-old white male shooting and killing six women of Asian descent and two others in March 2021 at massage parlors around Atlanta with names like "Youngs Asian Massage." Even George Takei, the beloved Japanese American actor from Star Trek who played Mr. Sulu on the USS Enterprise, appeared in several interviews and complained of the charged atmosphere. He said it was so dangerous to even go for a walk that he tried to restrict his walks to very early in the morning before sunrise.

Antagonism towards Jews remained widespread in the US and seemed to be growing increasingly crude in its expression. According to the ADL, anti-Semitic attacks increased 34 percent in 2021 over 2020, marking an all-time recorded high in the US.[162] The rising antisemitism was sufficiently alarming for American Jews to consider emigrating out of the US, as *The Washington Post* reported in December 2022: "An atmosphere that experts say began as a shock with the 2016 election of Donald Trump and his comments against religious and racial minorities has matured, taken root and for some led to serious consideration or action toward emigrating. Warm pride in Jewish parts of the national zeitgeist such as 'Seinfeld' has given way to cold calculations about *what if.*"[163]

A week after announcing his 2024 presidential candidacy in November 2022, Trump publicly dined at his Mar-a-Lago estate with the white supremacist commentator Nick Fuentes, who marched in Charlottesville in 2017, and the rapper Kanye West, who made a series of high-profile anti-Semitic statements including assailing "Jewish Zionists" and the "Jewish media" and vowing to go "death

---

162 "ADL Audit Finds Antisemitic Incidents in United States Reached All-Time High in 2021," ADL, April 25, 2022.
163 Michelle Boorstein, "'When was it too late?' Some U.S. Jews wonder about their place in America," *The Washington Post,* December 29, 2022.

con 3 On JEWISH PEOPLE."[164] Fuentes founded the America First Political Action Conference (AFPAC) attended by politicians including Marjorie Taylor Greene, denied the Holocaust,[165] exclaimed during a rant against Muslims that it was "time to kill the globalists,"[166] and viewed "America's 'white demographic core' as central to its identity."[167] Speaking on Alex Jones' show alongside Fuentes a few days after meeting with Trump, West, or as he called himself, "Ye," declared loudly and proudly, "I do love Hitler," "I also love Nazis," and "The Holocaust is not what happened."[168] West's statements had an immediate effect, with American Jewish cemeteries vandalized with swastikas and messages reading "Kanye was rite."[169] Trump continued to make statements about Jews after leaving the presidency, such as his November 2021 claim that "The biggest change I've seen in Congress is Israel literally owned Congress…Ten years ago, 15 years ago, and it was so powerful…and today it's almost the opposite."[170] In October 2022, he warned American Jews that they need to "get their act together" before "it is too late!" and give Trump more praise for his Israel policies.[171]

---

164 "Kanye West Threatens to Go 'Death Con 3 on Jewish People,'" *Haaretz*, October 9, 2022.

165 Maeve Reston and Kristen Holmes, "Trump hosted Holocaust denier at Mar-a-Lago estate during visit with Kanye West, a week after announcing 2024 run," *CNN*, November 26, 2022.

166 David Moye, "Right-Wing Broadcaster Calls For Killing Of 'Globalists At CNN,'" *HuffPost*, April 25, 2017.

167 "Nick Fuentes," Southern Poverty Law Center: https://www.splcenter.org/fighting-hate/extremist-files/individual/nick-fuentes

168 Danny Gallagher, "A Breakdown of Alex Jones' Squirmy Reactions to Kanye's Horrible 'I Like Hitler' Tirade," *Dallas Observer*, December 2, 2022.

169 Paul Best, "'Kanye Was Rite': Jewish Cemetery Vandalized With Swastikas," *Vice News*, November 16, 2022.

170 Ron Kampeas, "Trump: Until recently Israel 'literally owned Congress' — and that was a good thing," *Jewish Telegraph Agency*, November 1, 2021.

171 Paul LeBlanc, "Trump complains American Jews don't appreciate his moves on Israel, drawing criticism," *CNN*, October 17, 2022.

The ADL and other organizations tracking online hate also pointed to the white South African Silicon Valley corporate leader Elon Musk's purchase of Twitter in October 2022 as increasing anti-Semitic expression. In the two weeks following Musk's takeover and promise to restore "free speech" on the platform, anti-Semitic posts rose 61 percent, and slurs against Blacks tripled.[172] Musk, the world's richest man, seemed to be identifying with predator identity, describing the Jewish American military official Alexander Vindman, who testified against Trump at his first impeachment trial, as "puppet & puppeteer,"[173] declaring that Jewish financier George Soros "hates humanity" and "wants to erode the very fabric of civilization,"[174] and asserting that it was the "actual truth" that Jewish communities push "hatred against whites" and seek the immigration of "hordes of minorities."[175] He also called for Dr. Anthony Fauci to be prosecuted,[176] suggested that Nancy Pelosi's husband was attacked by a gay lover and not a politically-inspired assassin,[177] and tweeted a meme image of a white male waving the American flag courageously resisting a shadowy faceless figure representing the "left" or "establishment" featuring an Islamic crescent and star superimposed on a rainbow LGBTQ pride flag, a sickle and hammer, and a "Black Lives Matter" emblem.[178]

---

172 Sheera Frenkel and Kate Conger, "Hate Speech's Rise on Twitter Is Unprecedented, Researchers Find," *The New York Times*, December 2, 2022.
173 "Elon Musk calls Jewish US Army officer 'puppet & puppeteer,'" *Jerusalem Post*, November 28, 2022.
174 Elon Musk, Twitter.com, May 15, 2023.
175 Allison Morrow, "With antisemitic tweet, Elon Musk reveals his 'actual truth,'" *CNN*, November 17, 2023.
176 Ivana Saric, "Lawmakers react to Musk's call to prosecute Fauci," *Axios*, December 12, 2022.
177 Casey Tolan, Curt Devine, Scott Bronstein, and Daniel A. Medina, "'Absolutely no evidence:' Police, FBI affidavit debunk salacious conspiracy about Pelosi attack pushed by conservatives," *CNN*, October 31, 2022.
178 Elon Musk, Twitter.com, December 28, 2022.

Chapter 9 Crisis, Reckoning, and the Road to 2024

As noted above, Biden's presidency was characterized by a pluralist identity which was trying to both undo the effects of predator identity and "right the ship" for the future in pushing the nation to live up to the ideals of the Founding Fathers concerning inclusivity, equality, democracy, justice, and the rule of law. At the same time, amid a multitude of challenges facing all Americans, the adherents of predator identity, who had found their enduring leader in Trump, continued to broadly assail the political, governmental, media, economic, medical, and academic "establishment." They blamed the "establishment" for adversely and corruptly transforming the country, for example through immigration, diversity and inclusion policies, and prosecuting legal cases such as against the January 6 rioters and Trump himself.

One early test for the nation in Biden's presidency was how the murder case of George Floyd would be handled by the authorities. In a historic decision in April 2021, the Minneapolis policeman Derek Chauvin was convicted for the murder of George Floyd. Not only had the trial featured senior officials like the Minneapolis chief of police testifying against Chauvin, but it was one of the few times that a policeman had been convicted of murder after causing someone's death.[179] The person who oversaw the trial was Keith Ellison, the first Muslim elected to Congress who went on to become Minnesota's Attorney General. Ellison, who was sworn into Congress using Jefferson's Quran, was also the first Muslim elected to a statewide office in the US. When he first saw the video of Floyd's killing, Ellison said, "Even though I have been working on police accountability and brutality issues for years, I was still shocked. I was still blown away by the inhumanity of what I saw."[180] And yet he noted that the Minneapolis police department's first statement—"Man Dies After Medical Incident During Police Interaction"—made no mention that officers had pinned Floyd to the ground or put their knee on his neck. In assuming control of the trial, Ellison ensured that no "whitewashing" of the killing occurred. When the trial began, Ellison likened seeing Chauvin in court to Hannah Arendt's concept of "the banality of evil." "He looked like a relatively small man," Ellison said, "I bet he didn't weigh 140lb. Here's this guy who acted so monstrously: it's just a man, not a very big one."[181]

Ellison affirmed that the trial, which featured witnesses giving their testimony, such as the teenager who recorded the video of the killing and breaking down in tears, "restored my faith in humanity... I'm going to remember the courage of those people who stopped for a complete stranger...No one on that scene knew George Floyd, but they all stopped and did what they could for him." Speaking of Floyd's family, Ellison described "their dignity, how beautiful they were, how kind they were."[182] American society had a loss of "trust"

---

179 Shaila Dewan, "Few Police Officers Who Cause Deaths Are Charged or Convicted," *The New York Times*, September 24, 2020.
180 David Smith, "'It looked like Chauvin would get away with it':
Minnesota's top attorney on how he won justice for George Floyd's family,"
The Guardian, June 1, 2023.
181 Ibid.
182 Amir Vera and Omar Jimenez, "Minnesota AG Says Derek Chauvin Case Restored His Faith in Humanity," *CNN*, April 26, 2021.

on race issues and the police, he stated, which was "fundamental to democracy, it's fundamental to the idea of whether we have human rights for everyone. We say 'liberty and justice for all' at the end of the Pledge of Allegiance, and we mean it. But you've got to put something behind that." Ellison said that he did not believe that the verdict itself represented justice "Because justice implies true restoration…But it is accountability, which is the first step towards justice." For Ellison, it was a process toward achieving the kind of pluralist equality promised by the ideals of the Founding Fathers.

Despite the challenges the nation faced, Ellison, author of the book *Break the Wheel: Ending the Cycle of Police Violence* (2023), was optimistic: "it's sad but it's true: the people who killed George Floyd were a multiracial group. There was one Black officer, one Hmong officer, and two white officers. But the people who stood up for George Floyd were a multiracial group too. There was a young white woman who was a firefighter, two young white teenagers, a 61-year-old African American man, a 17-year-old Black girl. It was a mixed group and, if you look at the protests, they were multiracial. I'm not pessimistic. We can move forward but we've got to try to take stock of the lessons that are available to be learned."[183]

There was no doubt that mainstream America was now dealing in a much more direct way with its own history concerning minorities and episodes of violence that had been overlooked or ignored in the telling of US history. When we were reading American history for *Journey into America*, we studied numerous episodes of brutality, such as the epidemic of lynchings, but one event stood out as among the worst instances of racist violence—the total destruction in 1921 of America's wealthiest Black neighborhood, known as "Black Wall Street," in Tulsa, Oklahoma, by a white mob of 10,000. Airplanes

---

183 David Smith, "'It looked like Chauvin would get away with it': Minnesota's top attorney on how he won justice for George Floyd's family," *The Guardian*, June 1, 2023.

dropped explosives on Black citizens, and officially 39 people were killed, but estimates ran to as many as 300 and even 3,000. At the time of writing over a decade ago, this massacre was not well known in mainstream America, but in the era of Black Lives Matter, it attained national prominence. In May 2021, Viola Fletcher, a 107-year-old survivor of the massacre, testified before Congress about it, bringing the horrors of that day alive for the nation in an appeal for justice: "I still see Black men being shot, and Black bodies lying in the street. I still smell smoke and see fire. I still see Black businesses being burned. I still hear airplanes flying overhead. I hear the screams. I live through the Massacre every day...I am 107 years old and have never seen justice. I pray that one day I will. I have been blessed with a long life—and have seen the best and worst of this country. I think about the horrors inflicted upon Black people in this country every day."[184]

At the 100th anniversary of the massacre in June 2021, President Biden traveled to Tulsa and spoke at a commemoration attended by Fletcher and other survivors as well as Black leaders like Jesse Jackson, stating, "My fellow Americans, this was not a riot. This was a massacre, among the worst in our history, but not the only one. And for too long, forgotten by our history." Speaking about the rebirth or second founding of the Ku Klux Klan around that same period, Biden, the second Catholic president in US history after Kennedy, noted, "the Klan was founded just six years before the horrific destruction here in Tulsa. And one of the reasons why it was founded was because of guys like me, who were Catholic...Millions of white Americans belonged to the Klan, and they weren't even embarrassed by it; they were proud of it." America was a "great nation," he said, and "great nations...come to terms with their dark sides." Linking

---

184 "Written Testimony of Mother Viola Fletcher, United States House of Representatives, Subcommittee on the Constitution, Civil Rights, and Civil Liberties, Wednesday, May 19, 2021": https://docs.house.gov/meetings/JU/JU10/20210519/112648/HHRG-117-JU10-Wstate-FletcherV-20210519.pdf

past and present, he vowed to take steps to empower and elevate the Black community, work for racial justice, and stated that according to US intelligence, "terrorism from white supremacy is the most lethal threat to the homeland today."[185]

Steps were also being taken to commemorate the victims of lynchings, with the first memorial dedicated to the subject, the National Memorial for Peace and Justice, opening in 2018 in Alabama. In the fall of 2016, the first national museum dedicated to African American history and culture, the Smithsonian's National Museum of African American History and Culture, had opened in Washington, situated on the National Mall adjacent to the Washington Monument.

Yet, despite the prominence of the discussion about race in the US after 2020, nearly two-thirds of Black Americans in a 2023 study felt "that their community received more negative coverage than other racial and ethnic groups," and around four in 10 "said that the media not only stereotyped Black people" but that they observed "racist and racially insensitive coverage sometimes or fairly often."[186] Additionally, in a 2024 study, 75 percent of Black Americans said they had experienced racial discrimination[187] and 67 percent believed the US political system was "designed to hold Black people back, either a great deal or a fair amount."[188]

Controversy continued to rage about the teaching of US history, especially the role, interpretation, and legacy of slavery. By May

185 "Remarks by President Biden Commemorating the 100th Anniversary of the Tulsa Race Massacre," The White House, June 1, 2021: https://bidenwhitehouse.archives.gov/briefing-room/speeches-remarks/2021/06/02/remarks-by-president-biden-commemorating-the-100th-anniversary-of-the-tulsa-race-massacre/
186 Edwin Rios, "Majority of Black Americans say they are depicted unfairly in news – study," *The Guardian*, September 27, 2023.
187 Kiana Cox, "1. Racial discrimination shapes how Black Americans view their progress and U.S. institutions," Pew Research Center, June 15, 2024.
188 Kiana Cox, "Most Black Americans Believe U.S. Institutions Were Designed To Hold Black People Back," Pew Research Center, June 15, 2024.

2021, some 15 states had introduced bills that would legally restrict how race could be taught amidst the backlash against approaches like critical race theory and the 1619 Project.[189] By the following month, critical race theory had been banned in six states, with more set to follow. Responses to the 1619 Project included Texas introducing a bill to establish the "Texas 1836 Project" to promote "patriotic education" and offer a "presentation of the history of this state's founding and foundational principles."[190] While Biden abolished Trump's 1776 Commission hours after being inaugurated as president, the debates about identity and history that it was part of and further provoked persisted.

The Challenges Facing the US

When *Journey into America* was being written, the United States was still seen as the undisputed superpower of the world; while working on this present book over a decade after *Journey into America's* initial publication, I became acutely aware of the dramatic downturn in the fortunes of the US. Bookshops prominently displayed books expounding the theme of "The End of the American Empire." Serious commentators were not holding back. Nobel Prize-winning economist Joseph Stiglitz said the coronavirus crisis had left the US looking like a third-world country, and *The Atlantic* called the US "a failed state."[191] Respectable economists like Jeffrey Sachs, pastor-scholars like Chris Hedges, and more loyal than the king immigrant commentators like Fareed Zakaria all publicly announced the passing of the great power status of the US and listed its failings. And there was worse to come: UN experts warned of global famines of "Biblical

189 Julia Carrie Wong, "The Fight to Whitewash US History: 'A Drop of Poison is All You Need,'" *The Guardian*, May 25, 2021.
190 H.B. No. 2497: https://capitol.texas.gov/tlodocs/87R/billtext/pdf/HB02497F.pdf
191 George Packer, "We Are Living in a Failed State," *The Atlantic*, June 2020.

proportions" amidst the pandemic, and there was the distressing possibility of even more contagious coronavirus variants—or indeed the threat of a new disease entirely, the "next pandemic." Both contingencies, in addition to the devastating continuing effects of climate change, would further challenge the global leadership of the US.

With the US facing multiple problems, the climate of gloom was apparent. The county singer Oliver Anthony hit number one on the charts in 2023 with his song "Rich Men North of Richmond," in which he sings, "I've been sellin' my soul, workin' all day/ Overtime hours for bullshit pay" and "It's a damn shame what the world's gotten to/ For people like me and people like you." President Biden noted the previous year that Americans are "really, really down." Indeed, a July 2022 poll found that just 10 percent of the American public felt that the US was heading in the right direction. An NBC News poll conducted in early 2023 found that 71 percent of Americans said the country was going in the wrong direction, with NBC News pollsters noting, "We have never before seen this level of sustained pessimism in the 30-year-plus history of the poll."[192]

Coronavirus; gun violence; sexual assault—one in four American women reported rape or attempted rape[193]; the stark disparity between rich and poor—the top 10 percent of Americans owned roughly 70 percent of the nation's wealth while the bottom 50 percent held 2.5 percent of the wealth[194]; and the difficulty accessing health care particularly for poorer people—these were all urgent crises facing the country. A 2022 poll additionally found that an overwhelming 90 percent of Americans believed that mental health was

---

192 Chuck Todd, Mark Murray, Ben Kamisar, Bridget Bowman, and Alexandra Marquez, "Poll finds 71% of Americans believe country is on wrong track," *NBC News*, January 30, 2023.
193 Anne P. DePrince, "How Common Is Sexual Violence in the United States?," *Psychology Today*, July 18, 2022.
194 Anshu Siripurapu, "The U.S. Inequality Debate," Council on Foreign Relations, April 20, 2022.

a crisis facing the country and half reported a severe mental health crisis in their family.[195]

In 2021 and 2022, American life expectancy declined to its lowest point in 25 years due to COVID-19 and drug overdoses, decreasing from 78.8 years in 2019 to 76.4 years in 2022.[196] While it increased to 77.5 years in 2023, it was still not at pre-COVID levels. By the start of 2024, the coronavirus had killed 1.1 million Americans (or one in 500 people in the country) and infected 100 million, with 1,500 Americans still dying every week of the disease.[197] Experts stated that the death toll was estimated to be 16 percent higher than the official numbers.[198] In terms of drug fatalities, in 2022, there were 110,000 deaths from drug overdoses, 70 percent of which were caused by the opioid fentanyl.[199]

During our fieldwork for *Journey into America*, which we carried out towards the end of the 2000s era of excess and consumerism symbolized by figures like Paris Hilton, we explored the toll, particularly on young women, of pressures to adhere to beauty standards promoted by the media which many felt had the potential to lead to financial success and fame. Female converts to Islam commonly reported such pressures as factoring into their decision to convert. Since then, a generation has grown up raised on social media, which has only exacerbated these tendencies. In 2021, for example, the *Wall Street Journal* published internal Facebook documents showing that

195 Deidre McPhillips, "90% of US adults say the United States is experiencing a mental health crisis, CNN/KFF poll finds," *CNN*, October 5, 2022.
196 "US life expectancy is at its lowest in 25 years," *BBC News*, December 22, 2022.
197 Mary Kekatos, "Why are 1,500 Americans still dying from COVID every week?," *ABC News*, January 10, 2024.
198 Melody Schreiber, "Covid death toll in US likely 16% higher than official tally, study says," *The Guardian*, February 21, 2024.
199 "At last, a convincing explanation for America's drug-death crisis," *The Economist*, December 7, 2023.

company research found that its Instagram app was harmful to teens, particularly teen girls. Facebook researchers noted, "Thirty-two percent of teen girls said that when they felt bad about their bodies, Instagram made them feel worse," while the researchers reported that fourteen percent of American boys said that Instagram made them feel worse about themselves.[200] From 2000 to 2020, the number of female Americans ages 15 to 24 committing suicide rose by 87 percent, with most of the increase occurring after 2007, and the number of suicides by male Americans ages 15 to 24 also rose, but not nearly as starkly.[201] In 2023, the US recorded its highest-ever number of suicides, 50,000, superseding the nation's second-highest total of 49,449, recorded in 2022.[202] Suicide is now the number two cause of death for Americans under 35 years of age, with calls to the national suicide helpline 988 increasing by 100,000 per month in 2023.[203]

The problem of the police shooting unarmed people has continued—a study released in 2022 showed that nearly one-third of all people killed by US police in the past seven years were trying to run away in encounters which often began at traffic stops.[204] Mass shootings also showed no signs of slowing and not infrequently were marked as national tragedies. In May 2022, Payton Gendron, an 18-year-old male upset over the "great replacement" of whites, opened fire at a predominantly Black supermarket in Buffalo, NY, shooting 13 and killing 10. He adopted his ideology and murderous

200 Georgia Wells, Jeff Horwitz, and Deepa Seetharaman, "Facebook Knows Instagram Is Toxic for Teen Girls, Company Documents Show," *The Wall Street Journal*, September 14, 2021.
201 Matthew F. Garnett, Sally C. Curtin, and Deborah M. Stone, "Suicide Mortality in the United States, 2000–2020," CDC, NCHS Data Brief No. 433, March 2022.
202 Will Vernon, "Suicide is on the rise for young Americans, with no clear answers," *BBC News*, April 11, 2024.
203 Ibid.
204 Sam Levin, "'Hunted': One in Three People Killed by US Police Were Fleeing, Data Reveals," *The Guardian*, July 28, 2022.

plan from Brenton Tarrant, the perpetrator of the 2019 New Zealand Christchurch massacre of Muslims, calling his manifesto "You Wait for a Signal While Your People Wait for You," after a section in Tarrant's manifesto. Both killers cited Anders Breivik, the white supremacist Norwegian terrorist who in 2011 murdered 77 and injured 319 in and around Oslo for their perceived support of Muslim immigration.[205] While Gendron blamed Jews, Muslims, and Latinos for also being "replacers," he said he targeted Black Americans in this particular instance because "I can't possibly attack all groups at once so might as well target one."[206]

Gendron's concern about "replacement" was passing from online far-right spaces to being openly discussed in the media. Popular news figures like Tucker Carlson, cable television's top-rated host, warned of the "great replacement" of whites by non-white immigrants, discussing the so-called "theory" over 400 times on his Fox News show by spring 2022.[207]

Only ten days after Gendron's massacre, another 18-year-old male carried out a separate abhorrent act of violence, a mass shooting at Robb Elementary School in Uvalde, Texas, killing 19 innocent children and two teachers. This massacre was the most violent school attack the nation had seen in a decade since the 2012 mass shooting at Sandy Hook Elementary in Connecticut. While in the case of Uvalde, the killer did not seem motivated by white supremacy, as a young male "loner" facing possible mental health problems and alienation and deeply involved and participating in online forums that celebrated guns and extreme violence, his case fits into a larger

---

205 Jeff Sharlet, "The Terrifying Familiarity of the Buffalo Shooting Suspect's Extremist Screed," *Vanity Fair*, May 17, 2022.
206 Samuel Breslow, "The Buffalo shooter murdered Black people. His screed also oppresses Jews. Here's what it says," *Forward*, May 17, 2022.
207 Nicholas Confessore and Karen Yourish, "A Fringe Conspiracy Theory, Fostered Online, Is Refashioned by the G.O.P.," *The New York Times*, May 15, 2022.

cultural pattern.[208] A 2023 Secret Service study of 173 mass casualty attacks, most using guns, determined that "nearly 93% of assailants had dealt with a personal issue prior to their attack, whether it be divorce, health problems, or issues at school or work, and that 10% of assailants behind mass casualty events between 2016 and 2020 died by suicide."[209] While facing personal crises is something that happens to human beings wherever they live, as Josh Horwitz, co-director of the Johns Hopkins Center for Gun Violence Solutions, attested, "When you compare what is going on in the US to other countries, the one thing that they don't necessarily have that we have is just such easy access to firearms."[210] Gun sales reached a record 23 million in 2020, and one in five households in the US bought a gun between 2020 and 2022.[211] Horwitz said that the reason for the purchases is precisely Noam Chomsky's definition of American identity in his interview in *Journey into America*: fear. "People are afraid," Horwitz affirmed, "and they want to quell that fear by buying a gun."[212]

In January 2023, a six-year-old boy in Virginia shot his teacher in a near-fatal attack following an "altercation" in which the boy pulled a gun out of his backpack and pointed it at his teacher, and the teacher tried to confiscate it from him.[213] Researchers reported that this was not the first time six-year-old students were involved in shootings

---

208 See "Texas elementary school shooting: What do we know so far?," *Associated Press*, June 3, 2022.
209 Nadine Yousif, "Why number of US mass shootings has risen sharply," *BBC News*, March 28, 2023.
210 Ibid.
211 Ibid.; "One in Five American Households Purchased a Gun During the Pandemic," NORC at the University of Chicago: https://www.norc.org/research/library/one-in-five-american-households-purchased-a-gun-during-the-pande.html
212 Nadine Yousif, "Why number of US mass shootings has risen sharply," *BBC News*, March 28, 2023.
213 Erum Salam, "Virginia teacher who was shot by six-year-old tried to confiscate gun—report," *The Guardian*, January 9, 2023.

in the US, with other cases including a "fatal shooting of a fellow student in 2000 in Michigan and shootings that injured other students in 2011 in Texas and 2021 in Mississippi."[214] The Johns Hopkins professor Daniel W. Webster, who studies gun violence, attested that "A six-year-old gaining access to a loaded gun and shooting him or herself or someone else, sadly, is not so rare."[215] There appeared to be no limits to the violence. In spite of these trends, no serious efforts were made to curtail the purchase and distribution of guns.

Such social problems require a sober, sustained, and united approach to solve, but a divided America torn between the identities made it difficult to address its challenges. Effectively addressing urgent global crises like climate change would also not be possible without the full support of the American nation. Yet climate change and its real dangers to life on earth were still being seen through a partisan lens. Americans, furthermore, had become aware of how vulnerable they were without a national health program when the coronavirus came, and the issue of health care remained among the most divisive in domestic politics. Consensus and support were also needed on the issue of how to deal with China, which had emerged aggressively promoting its power and position and aspired to global leadership. Right-wing and authoritarian movements in Europe and beyond would also demand a coherent US response on the world stage.

Indeed, the US faced many foreign policy challenges. The war on terror continued around the world, and while Biden pulled US troops from Afghanistan, finally ending the longest war in US history, the future was uncertain in the Central and South Asian region as the Taliban assumed control of the country. The withdrawal itself descended into chaos—with the Taliban at the gates of Kabul, the US focused on evacuations, airlifting over 100,000 Afghans and over

---

214 Maya Yang and Associated Press, "Shooting of teacher by six-year-old a red flag for US, says mayor," *The Guardian*, January 8, 2023.
215 Ibid.

5,000 Americans out of the country in just 17 days. Images on television of soldiers and civilians scrambling to board the huge American planes at Kabul airport were eerily reminiscent of the ignominious American flight from Saigon. Afghans who clung to the transport plane as it picked up speed to take off were seen to be falling from the sky as it gained altitude. Conceptually, the defeat of America after two decades, thousands of lives, and trillions of dollars, was on an epic scale. It was up there with the catastrophic defeat of the British in the First Anglo-Afghan War in the nineteenth century. The US had spent more in Afghanistan than on the Marshall Plan to reconstruct Europe after the Second World War,[216] but in the end it was for naught. The manner of the US abandonment of Afghanistan was clearly a failure for the US and for President Joe Biden, who oversaw it. Yet to Biden, it woefully appeared to signify little.

The US also faced a transformed global geopolitical situation following Russia's invasion of Ukraine in February 2022. After launching the invasion and reportedly intending to change the regime in Kyiv and install a puppet ruler in less than a week, Russia suffered one defeat after another. Having lost most of its advanced equipment, it was forced to rely on obsolete T-62 tanks from the 1960s. The war led to a catastrophic loss of legitimacy for Putin and rising internal tension as the US rapidly spent billions of dollars aiding the Ukrainian resistance effort. Nearly every US company engaged in Russia, such as McDonalds, immediately cut off contact with the country, and the US-led economic sanctions effectively were designed to sever the world's largest country from the global economy. When Ukrainian President Volodymyr Zelenskyy addressed a joint session of the US Congress in December 2022 and delivered a rousing Churchillian speech, he was given a hero's welcome by both parties, a rarity in a bitterly divided Washington. Biden successfully maintained a united

---

216 Craig Whitlock, *The Afghanistan Papers: A Secret History of the War* (New York: Simon and Schuster, 2021), p. 30.

NATO and European front against Putin and worked to convince countries like China and India to put their own pressure on Russia. NATO even fast-tracked membership for Finland and Sweden.

The US After October 7

With Iran reeling from a brutally-suppressed internal revolt against its clerical dictatorship and China's growth slowing to a trickle while its population started to contract, the American-dominated Western alliance reached its most formidable position since the Soviet Union collapsed. With the exception of the Afghanistan withdrawal, Biden had exceeded just about everyone's expectations as president. But then came October 7 and Gaza. If the effects of the Israeli war against Hamas in Gaza are unpredictable in the Middle East and the world at large, they are equally so within the US. It is uncertain what long-term effects Gaza will have on US politics and society, but it was already apparent several months into the conflict that they could be profound. As in other countries such as European ones, as discussed in *Journey into Europe*, flare-ups in the Israeli-Palestinian conflict can impact relations between Jews and Muslims and between Jewish and Muslim minorities and the majority population. In the US, there was already a marked rise in antisemitism, for example, in the wake of the fighting between Israel and Palestinians in the spring of 2021, with Jonathan Greenblatt, the head of the Anti-Defamation League, warning of a "blitzkrieg of anti-Semitic acts across the country."[217]

Gaza was yet another level, both in terms of the intensity and devastation of the war itself, for which South Africa took Israel to the International Court of Justice on the charge of perpetuating a genocide. Gaza exacerbated pre-existing social cleavages in the US and provoked passionate reactions and debates. There was a concurrent

---

217 Erin Burnett Out Front, "CEO of ADL: Seeing a 'Blitzkrieg of Anti-Jewish' Acts Across US," *CNN*, May 24, 2021.

increase in both antisemitism and Islamophobia, which authorities and social and political leaders struggled to contain. Students across American campuses took the lead and, risking the wrath of the authorities, protested on behalf of the Palestinians in Gaza.

Many Americans, having been through the turmoil of 2020 and the George Floyd protests, saw the struggle of the Palestinians in similar terms as a question of justice, oppression, and human rights and demanded the US alter its customary relationship with Israel and exert its influence to stop the killing. Many Muslims, a core constituency who had helped elect Biden and were key to his victory in places like Michigan, indicated that Gaza was a red line for continuing support, and Arab and Muslim leaders organized a movement to vote "uncommitted" against Biden in the presidential primary in February 2024 to register their opposition. This campaign yielded over 100,000 votes in Michigan and more than half of the Democratic votes in Dearborn, an important Arab American center in which we conducted fieldwork. During fieldwork for *Journey into America,* Muslims in different parts of the country often told us that they endeavored to become more involved in politics and lobbying in an effort to alter US policy towards the Muslim world, the conduct of the "war on terror," and policy towards countries like Israel. Here, they were making their voices heard on the issue of Gaza.

They were also driven by the urgency of the threat of Islamophobia, with reports of anti-Muslim and anti-Palestinian discrimination and hate rising by around 180 percent in the three months following the Hamas attack on October 7, 2023.[218] Dearborn itself was referred to as "America's Jihad Capital" in a *Wall Street Journal* op-ed in February 2024.[219] There were shocking incidents of violence,

---

218 Kanishka Singh, "Anti-Muslim incidents jump in US amid Israel-Gaza war," *Reuters*, January 29, 2024.
219 Steven Stalinsky, "Welcome to Dearborn, America's Jihad Capital," *The Wall Street Journal*, February 2, 2024.

such as the October 2023 fatal stabbing of a six-year-old Palestinian American boy, Wadea Al-Fayoume, near Chicago by his white male landlord, Joseph Czuba, who was upset over the conflict, yelling, "you Muslims must die." Czuba, a listener of conservative talk radio who believed he was in danger from Palestinians and was worried about a "national day of jihad," stabbed Wadea 26 times and stabbed Wadea's mother, Hanaan Shahin, over a dozen times, although she survived the attack.[220] In Burlington, Vermont, in November 2023, three male Palestinian college students studying in the US, two of whom were wearing the Palestinian keffiyeh scarf, were shot by a white man. Hisham Awartani, who was paralyzed in the shooting, said he was wearing the keffiyeh both because it was cold and also because "we felt as Palestinians, during this time period, it's important for us to show our identity and to show that we exist and that we're human."[221] At my own university, American University, a Palestinian staff member received a letter reading, "Go back where you came from. You might get lucky with a missile, and meet your Allah sooner! Death to all Palestinians!"[222] In January 2024, a Jewish middle school teacher in Georgia threatened his students after a Muslim student asked why he had an Israeli flag displayed, saying they found it offensive because of "Israelis killing (Palestinians)"—the teacher responded by screaming "You motherf***ing piece of s**t! I'll kick your a**! I should cut your motherf***ing off!...I will drag her by the back of my car and cut her f***ing head off for disrespecting my Jewish flag," adding that

---

220 David Struett, "Plainfield man fatally stabbed 6-year-old Muslim boy after listening to conservative talk radio, prosecutors say," *Chicago Sun-Times*, October 16, 2023; Angela Yang, Dennis Romero, Marlene Lenthang, and Mirna Alsharif, "6-year-old Palestinian American boy is killed in anti-Muslim attack in Illinois, authorities say," *NBC News*, October 16, 2023.
221 "Palestinian American survivors speaks out on Vermont shooting," *NBC News*, January 17, 2024.
222 Susan H. Greenberg, "FBI Investigates Anti-Palestinian Message at American University," *Inside Higher Ed*, October 31, 2023.

he would "slit her f***ing throat."[223] In June 2024, a woman in Texas attempted to drown a Palestinian American girl in a swimming pool after telling the child's mother, who was wearing a hijab, that she was not American.[224]

According to the ADL, there were more anti-Semitic incidents reported in the two months after October 7 in the US than any other such period since it began tracking in 1979—such acts were up 337 percent.[225] Turmoil over antisemitism roiled American college campuses. There were threats against Jewish students, for example, at Cornell, where a student threatened to "'bring an assault rifle to campus and shoot all you'…to 'stab' and 'slit the throat' of Jewish men, rape Jewish women and throw their bodies off a cliff, and behead Jewish babies."[226] At American University, Jewish students sued the school for failing to take action against antisemitism, with an Israeli Jewish student saying, "he's been spit on multiple times and that someone scribbled 'Hitler was right' on a poster for his piano recital."[227] Professors across the country were suspended and probed over comments regarding Gaza, Hamas, Palestine, and Israel[228] and the presidents of Harvard and the University of Pennsylvania were removed after they declined to state in a US Congressional hearing "that calling for

223 Dianne Gallagher, "Teacher accused of threatening to behead student over Israeli flag comments 'no longer an employee' at school, district says," *CNN*, January 4, 2024.

224 Kelly Rissman, "Texas woman accused of trying to drown 3-year-old Palestinian American girl in swimming pool," *The Independent*, June 24, 2024.

225 "US antisemitism up 337% since October 7 in all-time record, ADL says," *Times of Israel*, December 12, 2023.

226 Erum Salam, "Cornell student who allegedly made antisemitic threats to appear in court," *The Guardian*, November 1, 2023.

227 Jessica Kronzer, "Complaint alleges American University failed to take action against antisemitism targeting Jewish students," *WTOP News*, January 17, 2024.

228 Andrew Hay, "US professors suspended, probed over Gaza war comments," *Reuters*, November 17, 2023.

the genocide of Jews would necessarily violate their code of conduct. Instead, they explained it would depend on the circumstances and conduct."[229] A third university president, of Columbia University, later resigned over her handling of the turmoil on campus. In Los Angeles, a Muslim college professor was charged "with involuntary manslaughter and battery in the death of a Jewish protester during demonstrations over the Israel-Hamas war."[230] The *Atlantic* declared in a cover story, "The Golden Age of American Jews is Ending."[231]

It was a time of great trial for the interfaith movement involving Jews and Muslims, with major initiatives promoting coexistence, such as a trip to Southern Spain and Morocco jointly organized by the Islamic Society of North America (ISNA) and the National Council of Synagogues (NCS) in early 2024 canceled due to the rising tensions.[232] Senior Rabbi Bruce Lustig of the Washington Hebrew Congregation, a pioneer of interfaith dialogue from 9/11 who we interviewed in *Journey into America*, told us with sorrow that since the Gaza conflict began, no Muslim, even those who used to visit frequently, had come to his synagogue. The US clearly needed bold and moral leadership to promote pluralism and heal divisions between communities at multiple levels of society. The Biden administration's announced framework after October 7 of fighting both Islamophobia and antisemitism concurrently was a correct approach—I have analyzed both as two sides of the same coin. Demonstrating its pluralist outlook, the Biden administration made it clear for the first time

229 Matt Egan and Donald Judd, "Harvard, Penn and MIT presidents under fire over 'despicable' testimony on antisemitism and genocide," *CNN*, December 6, 2023.
230 John Antczak and Julie Watson, "California professor charged with involuntary manslaughter in the death of Jewish demonstrator," *Associated Press*, November 16, 2023.
231 Franklin Foer, "The Golden Age of American Jews is Ending," *The Atlantic*, March 4, 2024.
232 Tom Gjelten, "A Cooling: Jewish-Muslim Interfaith Work after October 7 and Gaza," *Moment*, February 23, 2024.

"that Title VI of the Civil Rights Act of 1964 prohibits certain forms of antisemitism and Islamophobia."[233]

For adherents of predator identity, however, the Gaza war was yet another salvo in the "war on terror" and an illustration of the threat posed by Islam. Trump, who announced his reelection campaign for the presidency in November 2022, seized on the opportunity to announce that the "Muslim ban" would not only be reinstated should he win the presidency in 2024 but would be expanded—for example, it would now include anyone from Gaza.[234] Trump said that "ideological screening" would be instituted for all immigrants, and "if you don't like our religion…you are not getting in."[235] Anyone with "jihadist sympathies" would be deported, he said, and he promised to send immigration agents to "pro-jihadist demonstrations" to identify anyone violating these rules. Trump warned of an "invasion" of "millions and millions of people" coming into the US "from jails, and they're coming from prisons, and they're coming from mental institutions, and they're coming from insane asylums, and they're terrorists."[236] He accused Biden of having perpetuated a "vicious violation" of "our country" by having "transported the entire columns of fighting aged men—and they're all at a certain age, and you look at them, I said 'They look like warriors to me, something is going on that's bad…the United States is being overrun.'"[237]

---

233 Monica Alba and Peter Alexander, "Biden administration unveils new actions to combat antisemitism on college campuses," *NBC News*, October 30, 2023.

234 "Trump vows to expand Muslim ban and bar Gaza refugees if he wins presidency," *Associated Press*, October 17, 2023.

235 Ryan Bort, "Trump Says He'll Ban Immigrants Who 'Don't Like Our Religion,'" *Rolling Stone*, October 23, 2023.

236 Donald Trump, "Trump speaks on immigration during campaign visit to U.S.-Mexico border," *PBS Newshour*, YouTube.com, February 29, 2024.

237 Ibid.

Predator Identity and the Return of Trump

As in his previous campaigns, Trump's anti-Muslim messages in the 2024 election cycle fit into his larger anti-immigrant platform. Trump said on social media, "ILLEGAL IMMIGRATION IS POISONING THE BLOOD OF OUR NATION,"[238] a message he repeated at his rallies. When Biden's campaign likened the comments to Hitler's language in *Mein Kampf,* Trump said, "I never read 'Mein Kampf'…I know nothing about Hitler."[239] If elected in 2024, Trump promised to launch "the largest domestic deportation operation in American history," and Bannon vowed, "Mass deportations are going to start, if you don't like that, then don't vote for President Trump."[240] Trump officials like Stephen Miller advocated "building mass deportation camps,"[241] proposals similar to ideas discussed and feared concerning Arabs and Muslims after 9/11, as described in *Journey into America,* and evoking the Japanese internment policy during the Second World War. Trump also described his political enemies as "vermin" while warning about the "threat from within" the US, and promised that if elected again, he would be a dictator on "day one."[242] Appealing directly to primordial identity, Trump vowed, "To

238 Nikki McCann Ramirez, "Republicans Are Excusing Trump's Hitleresque 'Poison the Blood' Rhetoric," *Rolling Stone,* December 18, 2023.

239 Rebecca Shabad, "Trump on 'poisoning the blood' remarks: 'I never knew that Hitler said it,'" *NBC News,* December 22, 2023.

240 Isaac Arnsdorf, Nick Miroff, and Josh Dawsey, "Trump and allies plotting militarized mass deportations, detention camps," *The Washington Post,* February 21, 2024; Marita Vlachou, "Donald Trump Says Local Police Will Play Key Role In His Mass Deportation Plan," *Huff Post,* March 1, 2024.

241 Isaac Arnsdorf, Nick Miroff, and Josh Dawsey, "Trump and allies plotting militarized mass deportations, detention camps," *The Washington Post,* February 21, 2024.

242 Marianne LeVine, "Trump calls political enemies 'vermin,' echoing dictators Hitler, Mussolini," *The Washington Post,* November 13, 2023; David A. Graham, "Trump Says He'll Be a Dictator on 'Day One,'" *The Atlantic,* December 6, 2023.

achieve victory in this fight, just like in the battles of the past, we still need the hand of our Lord," and he asserted, "No one will be touching the Cross of Christ under the Trump Administration."[243] Trump's campaign video "God Made Trump," which he released just before the third anniversary of the January 6 attack and played at his rallies, depicted baby pictures of Trump over the narration, "On June 14, 1946, God looked down on his planned paradise and said, 'I need a caretaker,' so God gave us Trump."[244] Trump continued to state that the 2020 election was stolen from him and described prisoners convicted for involvement in the January 6 attack as "hostages."[245]

Not to be outdone, Florida Governor Ron DeSantis, who was among those challenging Trump for the 2024 Republican presidential nomination and seemed to have early momentum, promised to deport many more "illegals" than Trump would, attacked Trump for being too tolerant of gay rights and transgender people,[246] vowed to shoot immigrants breaking through the "border wall,"[247] and said that no Palestinian refugee should be admitted from Gaza because they "are all antisemitic."[248] DeSantis also minimized Putin's invasion of Ukraine as a "territorial dispute" amid an increasing Republican

---

243 Nathan Layne and Tim Reid, "Trump portrays 2024 race as a Christian battle, akin to D-Day," *Reuters*, February 24, 2024; Vivian Jones, "Trump vows to support Christians during Nashville speech: 'Bring back our religion,'" *The Tennessean*, February 22, 2024.
244 Donald J. Trump, "God Made Trump," Truth Social, January 5, 2024.
245 Adam Gabbatt, "Trump's novel take on January 6: calling convicted rioters 'hostages,'" *The Guardian*, January 13, 2024.
246 Kit Maher, Kristen Holmes, and Kaanita Iyer, "DeSantis campaign shares video slamming Trump's past vow to protect LGBTQ rights," *CNN*, July 2, 2023.
247 Steve Contorno and Kit Maher, "DeSantis pitches crackdown on illegal immigration in first major policy proposal of his campaign," *CNN*, June 27, 2023.
248 Stephen Groves, "DeSantis says US shouldn't take in Palestinian refugees from Gaza because they're 'all antisemitic,'" *Associated Press*, October 15, 2023.

swing against Ukraine funding, which was held up for months in the Republican-run House of Representatives, to Biden's alarm. Trump, for his part, called for all US aid to Ukraine to be paused "until federal agencies provided 'every scrap' of evidence they had on any business dealings from President Biden and Hunter Biden."[249] Despite no proof of any wrongdoing on the part of Biden or his family, the Republicans nevertheless initiated proceedings to impeach Biden for purported crimes—proceedings that they continued even after it was revealed in February 2024 that one of their key witnesses arguing that the Ukrainian energy firm Burisma paid bribes to the Bidens was found not only to have lied to the FBI but to have been fed information by Russian intelligence.[250]

It had seemed at certain points, for example, after January 6, that the Trumpian fever in America could have begun to break. Another such moment occurred following the 2022 midterm elections, which saw the Democrats gain seats in the Senate and only narrowly relinquish control of the House of Representatives. We must keep in mind that while individuals may embody an identity, such as Trump representing predator identity, the group around them has the ability to adjust if the leader shows signs of faltering. In the case of Trump, the Republicans began to identify younger alternative leaders to Trump in figures like DeSantis, who were equally zealous in their predatory expression—indeed, Muslim Guantanamo Bay detainees identified DeSantis as being involved in torture while serving at the prison with the US Navy.[251]

---

249 Kathryn Watson, "Where the Republican presidential candidates stand on Israel and Ukraine funding," *CBS News*, December 8, 2023.

250 Glenn Thrush and Alan Feuer, "Ex-Informant Accused of Lying About Bidens Said He Had Russian Contacts," *The New York Times*, February 20, 2024.

251 Kwan Wei Kevin Tan, "An ex-Guantanamo Bay detainee says he still remembers Ron DeSantis smiling at him from behind a fence while he was being force-fed: 'You cannot forget that,'" *Business Insider*, July 23, 2023.

DeSantis took a series of actions designed to assume the mantle of predator and primordial identity and thus win the presidency in 2024. He assembled a series of "hits" designed to resemble Trump's noted above, which caused outrage to the "liberals" and delight to supporters, such as his statement that all Palestinians from Gaza are anti-Semites. He declared that if elected president he would "start slitting throats" in the federal bureaucracy; announced that he would name a defense secretary who would also "slit some throats"; launched stunts like transporting immigrants to Martha's Vineyard and the Vice President's residence in Washington, D.C. and leaving them there to protest against Biden's border policies; declared a so-called "war on woke"; said of Dr. Fauci, "someone needs to grab that little elf and chuck him across the Potomac"; stated that slavery bestowed benefits on Black Americans and defended the inclusion of such assertions in school history curricula; and overhauled the Florida school curriculum more generally: "Videos that compare climate activists to Nazis, portray solar and wind energy as environmentally ruinous and claim that current global heating is part of natural long-term cycles will be made available to young schoolchildren in Florida."[252] With DeSantis leading the way, US lawmakers were furiously compiling lists of books to ban from school in order to protect students from the alleged sex, violence, and subject matter dealing with LGBT people they contained.

DeSantis was particularly known for his "Don't Say Gay" bill, which became Florida law and stipulated that public school teachers are not allowed to "encourage classroom discussion about sexual orientation or gender identity in primary grade levels."[253] This bill was inspired by the European far-right and leaders like Viktor Orbán

252 Oliver Milman, "Videos denying climate science approved by Florida as state curriculum," *The Guardian*, August 10, 2023.
253 Arwa Mahdawi, "Florida's 'don't say gay' law may sound vague—but its purpose is clear," *The Guardian*, July 2, 2022.

of Hungary—DeSantis' press secretary said, "we were watching the Hungarians" in shaping the bill.[254] When Disney came out against the bill, DeSantis removed Disney World's self-governing status and appointed Bridget Ziegler, co-founder of the far-right anti-LGBT "parental rights" group Moms for Liberty, to the board of the district overseeing Disney World's administration. Clearly predator identity was seeing threats in the gay and transgender communities—in November 2022 it was reported that US events featuring performers in drag were threatened or attacked at least 124 times during the year, with the most incidents occurring in Texas and North Carolina.[255] A mass shooting at one such event in November 2022, at Club Q in Colorado, killed five people and injured 17.

And yet, despite DeSantis' best efforts and those of other challengers like Nikki Haley, Trump's support proved to be enduring and his 2024 campaign was a juggernaut similar to his previous runs for office. Trump's 2024 campaign theme could be summed up in one word: revenge. He outlined this message in his 2023 address to CPAC: "I am your warrior, I am your justice, and for those who have been wronged and betrayed, I am your retribution, I am your retribution." As 2024 began, it was clear that Trump's legal troubles—more than two dozen lawsuits and investigations had been opened against him[256]—would be a constant and potentially defining factor in the elections, particularly the 91 federal indictments he was facing for attempting to overthrow the results of the 2020 election and the January 6 attack and for taking highly classified documents from the White House to Mar-a-Lago.

---

254 Zack Beauchamp, "Ron DeSantis is following a trail blazed by a Hungarian authoritarian," *Vox*, April 28, 2022.
255 Ella Ceron, "US Drag Events Were Threatened, Attacked at Least 124 Times This Year," *Bloomberg*, November 23, 2022.
256 Josh Marcus and Louise Hall, "Here Are All 29 Lawsuits Trump is Facing Now that He's Left Office," *The Independent*, May 19, 2021.

There were also additional cases, such as the State of New York's case against Trump on the charge of illegally influencing the 2016 presidential election by paying hush money to Stormy Daniels and the State of Georgia's case against Trump and those aiding him on the charge of overthrowing the results of the election in Georgia under the Racketeering Influenced and Corrupt Organizations Act (RICO) designed to fight organized crime. Once again, however, the immense pressure Trump was under from the legal system only drove the sense among his supporters that he was unfairly being targeted by malign forces. Trump seamlessly linked his own legal problems with his vow to dismantle and replace the "deep state" or supposedly liberal government bureaucracy and institutions, describing the FBI, for example, as the "Gestapo."[257] "They're not after me," Trump said in December 2023 to supporters, "They're after you. I'm just standing in the way," and "We're engaged in a righteous crusade."[258] Trump told his followers, "'I take all these arrows for you and I'm so proud to take them…I'm being indicted for you,' outstretching his arms as if on a cross."[259] As Trump cleared the field of challengers in advance of an expected general election rematch with Joe Biden, it was clear that many agreed with him.

As it stood, if Trump returned to the White House, he could reverse Biden's pluralist steps and America would be marching in the opposite direction that Biden had taken. Biden himself raised the alarm as he geared up for the 2024 election, saying that journalists "personally told me if he wins, they will have to leave the country because he's threatened to put them in jail." Trump "embraces politi-

257 Ben Samuels, "Trump Compares 'Marxist Thugs' FBI to Gestapo, Germany's Nazi-era Secret Police," *Haaretz*, January 18, 2023.
258 Matthew Medsger, "Trump delivers wide-ranging speech to New Hampshire hockey arena," *Boston Herald*, December 16, 2023.
259 Vivian Jones, "Trump vows to support Christians during Nashville speech: 'Bring back our religion,'" *The Tennessean*, February 22, 2024.

cal violence," Biden warned, "No president since the Civil War has done that."[260]

Biden and the Three Identities

It is important to reiterate in this discussion of contemporary America and the three identities that people often do not exclusively reflect and embody one identity or the other but can change over time and display aspects of each concurrently. A good example is Ronald Reagan, who I have analyzed above in terms of primordial identity, but in truth, also displayed elements of both pluralist and predator identities. Reagan projected an affable humility, an embrace of immigrants, and a commitment to goodness and reasonableness, American values, and the American vision rooted in the Founding Fathers. Perhaps this could help explain Reagan's electoral dominance and enduring popularity—in his 1984 electoral victory, which is virtually incomprehensible in today's political environment, Reagan won every US state apart from his challenger Walter Mondale's home state of Minnesota. Reagan also projected American power, glory, a clear sense that enemies such as the Soviet Union were "evil" and that drastic and forceful measures were justified to fight them, and a platform for reviving American greatness. Trump took his "Make America Great Again" slogan from Reagan, dropping only Reagan's "Let's" which preceded it.

Biden is similarly complex. While he overtly embraces, and I have analyzed him in terms of pluralist identity, Biden has, at different points, reflected all three identities. In terms of primordial identity, he was public about his Christian faith—although the fact that Biden is Catholic, as noted above, added a nuance in appealing to primordial identity which is based in Protestantism. It was Biden's only Catholic

---

260 Ted Johnson, "'He's Threatened To Put Them In Jail': Joe Biden Tells Katie Couric That Journalists Have Told Him Of Their Fears If Donald Trump Returns To White House," *Deadline*, February 22, 2024.

predecessor as president, John F. Kennedy, who, even before Reagan, had revived Massachusetts Bay Colony Governor John Winthrop in describing the US as the "shining city on a hill." Kennedy thus demonstrated his adherence to central features of primordial identity while also seeking to open it up beyond Protestants, and enlarge American identity itself. Biden too referenced Winthrop in defining American identity as the "shining city on the hill,"[261] but after Trump won the presidency in 2016, lamented, "So much for the shining city on the hill."[262] Biden presented his 2020 campaign against Trump in religious terms, as seeking to "restore the soul of America." Biden's political rhetoric invoked, in accordance with primordial identity and similar to Reagan, moral, decent, and hard-working ordinary people who sought a fair shot at the American dream.

In terms of predator identity, Biden also at times showed signs of compromising his pluralist positions. He initially refused to raise Trump's historically low refugee admission cap of 15,000 before a strong reaction led him to reconsider and raise it, with analysts pointing to the fact that the initial decision was taken amidst concern "about the optics of a record number of undocumented immigrants arriving at the southern border."[263] Vice President Harris, tasked with handling immigration from Central America, bluntly told Guatemalans in a speech in Guatemala in June 2021, "Do not come. The United States will continue to enforce our laws and secure our border."[264] And while Biden had announced his plans to close the prison at Guantanamo Bay, like Obama, he failed to do so.

---

261 Lucy Madison, "Honoring slain police officer, Biden blasts 'twisted, perverted, knock-off jihadis,'" *CBS News*, April 24, 2013.

262 Allan Smith, "Joe Biden goes off on the 2016 campaign: 'So much for the shining city on the hill,'" *Business Insider*, December 8, 2016.

263 "Joe Biden Raises Trump Refugee Cap After Backlash," *BBC News*, May 4, 2021.

264 Lauren Egan, "Harris, in Guatemala, Warns Potential Migrants: 'Do Not Come,'" *NBC News*, June 7, 2021.

The "optics" of having large numbers of immigrants crossing the southern border nevertheless was a political source of criticism of the Biden administration, especially as migrant arrivals reached unprecedented levels following the end of Trump's first term. Indeed, Trump made the high immigration rates under Biden a centerpiece of his reelection campaign. Thousands of unaccompanied minors arrived, for example, who usually would be placed in shelters licensed by state child welfare authorities.[265] Yet Biden coped with the numbers by placing the children in detention facilities in places such as military bases and former oil worker camps, which had no such licenses. At the facility in Fort Bliss, Texas, employees reported that the migrant children were so distressed that "they are constantly monitored for incidents of self-harm, panic attacks and escape attempts," with the US government banning toothbrushes, nail clippers, pens, and pencils due to fears the children would commit suicide.[266] One migrant girl "cut herself in front of other children after learning that case managers had not spoken to her mother about her release."[267] At another facility, there were few activities for the children, and "what little outdoor recreation they do have takes place in unshaded areas where temperatures sometimes reach over 110 degrees."[268] The Department of Homeland Security (DHS) inspector general also reported in 2024 that over the previous five years, a time period that included Biden's presidency and the end of Trump's, tens of thousands of child migrants had failed to appear for court hearings, meaning that the US government had lost track of them. The inspector general explained, "Without an ability to monitor the location and status of [unaccom-

265 Camilo Montoya-Galvez, "U.S. reopening facility near southern border to house unaccompanied migrant children," *CBS News*, October 13, 2023.
266 Ibid.
267 Ibid.
268 Priscilla Alvarez, "Migrant kids describe raw food and extended stays at Texas temporary facility," *CNN*, August 10, 2021.

panied migrant children], ICE has no assurance [they] are safe from trafficking, exploitation, or forced labor."[269]

Then, in 2024, amid the presidential campaign, Biden barred migrants from claiming asylum entirely in the US if they had entered the country illegally at a time when illegal border crossings were reported to be over 2,500 per day—which they had been during the previous three years of Biden's presidency. If illegal crossings went below 1,500 per day, the US would then permit migrants to once again claim asylum.[270] To implement this law, Biden invoked the same provision in the 1952 Immigration and Nationality Act that Trump used for the "Muslim Ban." The law reads, "[W]henever the President finds that the entry of any aliens or of any class of aliens into the United States would be detrimental to the interests of the United States, he may by proclamation, and for such period as he shall deem necessary, suspend the entry of all aliens or any class of aliens as immigrants or nonimmigrants, or impose on the entry of aliens any restrictions he may deem to be appropriate."[271] Rights groups, including Amnesty International and the American Civil Liberties Union (ACLU), opposed Biden's action. Amnesty's director of Refugee and Migrant Rights, Amy Fischer, stated, "It's deeply disappointing to see President Biden so hellbent on dismantling human rights for people seeking asylum and implementing policies that are plainly illegal under international and refugee law."[272] The ACLU's director of policy and

---

269 Mike Levine, Lucien Bruggeman, and Laura Romero, "DHS watchdog warns of 'urgent issue' after immigration officials allegedly lose track of unaccompanied children," *ABC News*, August 20, 2024.

270 "Biden takes executive action to limit asylum seekers at Southern border," *NBC News*, YouTube.com, June 4, 2024: https://youtu.be/7M5JyI9-YNM?si=WQkX4wjYmOOoV2zo

271 "Understanding INA Section 212(f): The President's Authority to Suspend the Entry of Migrants," American Immigration Council, June 4, 2024: https://www.americanimmigrationcouncil.org/research/understanding-ina-section-212f-president-authority-suspend-entry-migrants

272 Sergio Martínez-Beltrán, "Biden's new executive order denies asylum

government affairs for border and immigration, Maribel Hernandez Rivera, called the new policy "a repeat of what President Trump did, that is just a repeat of cruel policies."[273]

The policy led to thousands of migrants massing in northern Mexico in unsafe and unsanitary conditions while attempting to secure US appointments on a glitch-plagued American government phone app.[274] Biden had already banned migrants from seeking asylum in the US if they did not first request refugee status in another country on their way to the US, which disqualified "most non-Mexican asylum seekers."[275] If migrants were found to not qualify for asylum and were returned to their countries, they were then banned for five years from returning to the US.

The clash of the identities on Biden's position was also revealed clearly in the Israel-Gaza war: his initial proclamation of support for Israel was total, but he was uncomfortable with the way the war was being conducted. To his credit, Biden urged Israeli Prime Minister Benjamin Netanyahu not to follow the path of revenge and anger, as the US did after 9/11. But Netanyahu ignored this sensible advice. The number of Palestinian civilians being killed, especially the women and children, and the devastation to property could not be hidden. The title "Genocide Joe" given to Biden by compatriot opponents of his policy was especially cruel, keeping in mind the emphasis on compassion and kindness that pluralist America is supposed to represent.

Biden's generous military support for the Israeli army did not waver, and his protestations to stop the war appeared feeble. As the war

claims to most migrants crossing the border unlawfully," *NPR*, June 4, 2024.
273 Ibid.
274 Mary Beth Sheridan, "Mexico faces humanitarian crisis as Biden migration policy kicks in," *The Washington Post*, May 13, 2023.
275 "Biden administration's new asylum restrictions explained," *CBS News*, YouTube.com, May 11, 2023: https://www.youtube.com/watch?v=n49Qd8o8vNc

dragged on, however, with the killing unabated and dying children shown 24/7 on TV news, Biden could neither ignore the outrage that was growing both nationally and internationally nor contain his pluralist impulse: he ordered that aid be air-dropped to the besieged Palestinians. His demand for a ceasefire became louder and firmer. Yet, like Obama and Guantanamo Bay, Biden was undoubtedly aware of how American predator identity, which tended to identify with Israel in the "war on terror" and against Islam and Palestinians, would interpret any perceived wavering of support for Israel, even in the face of such high levels of civilian killings. When Biden threatened to halt shipments of certain bombs and munitions to Israel, Republicans pounced—Trump declared that Biden had taken "the side of these terrorists"[276] while US Speaker of the House Mike Johnson attributed Biden's "abandoning Israel" to his wish not "to offend a big segment of his base...There's an actual pro-Hamas, pro-Palestinian wing of the Democratic Party."[277] The end result was the catastrophe befalling the people of Gaza, who endured more bombs in the first six months of the war alone than were dropped on London, Dresden, and Hamburg during the entirety of the Second World War.[278] An article published in the *Lancet* medical journal nine months into the war estimated that the death toll in Gaza could be as high as 186,000.[279] If this was indeed the case, reported Devi Sridhar, the chair of global

---

276 David Jackson, Sudiksha Kochi, Francesca Chambers, and Riley Beggin, "Trump and Republicans slam Biden over pledge to withhold weapons from Israel over Rafah," *USA Today*, May 9, 2024.

277 Mike Johnson, "Speaker Johnson on Biden Abandoning Israel: '100% Political,'" US Congressman Mike Johnson, Press Release, May 9, 2024: https://mikejohnson.house.gov/news/documentsingle. aspx?DocumentID=1390

278 Muhammed Enes Çallı, "Amount of Israeli bombs dropped on Gaza surpasses that of World War II," *Anadolu Ajansı*, June 4, 2024.

279 Rasha Khatib, Martin McKee, and Salim Yusuf, "Counting the dead in Gaza: difficult but essential," *The Lancet*, Vol. 404, No. 10449, 2024, pp. 237-238.

public health at the University of Edinburgh, then the death toll at the end of 2024 would be about 335,500 Palestinians killed.[280]

Additionally, however blustery Trump's rhetoric, when push came to shove, Trump avoided taking the US into new conflicts in his first term. Biden, in contrast, had tangled the United States in military adventures on two fronts, directly in the Middle East and indirectly in Ukraine. In the Middle East, as noted above, Israel and Gaza were part of the larger regional confrontation with Iran which grew increasingly perilous. In Ukraine particularly there was a danger of triggering a nuclear war. The Ukrainian resistance to Russia's widely condemned and brutal invasion was heroic, and Biden's backing of Ukraine principled, but as the war ground on year after year, Biden was criticized both for giving Ukraine too much aid, thus stretching out an unwinnable war, and also for not giving enough for Ukraine to win while setting too many conditions on the use of American weaponry. By 2024, both wars, as NPR reported, were "defining Biden's presidency and complicating his reelection bid."[281]

---

280 Devi Sridhar, "Scientists are closing in on the true, horrifying scale of death and disease in Gaza," *The Guardian*, September 5, 2024.
281 Greg Myre, "How 2 unexpected wars are defining Biden's presidency," *NPR*, June 11, 2024.

Chapter 10 The 2024 Election and the Triumph of Predator Identity

The run-up to the presidential elections in the summer of 2024 was full of drama. Amid the talk of civil war taking shape across the land came a shocking assassination attempt on Trump. As he prepared to speak at a large rally in Pennsylvania, a young shooter from the vantage point of a nearby rooftop fired several shots at Trump, one of which hit him in the ear. The near brush with death was close enough not only to shock Trump but also send a wave of sympathy throughout the country. It was a galvanizing moment in history. Two days later, the Republican convention in Milwaukee was like a love fest. Trump was not only being hailed as the presidential candidate; he was being crowned king. Had Trump undergone a Pauline change? From an angry man attacking every target in sight, he was now talking of unity and bringing people together. Yet within a few days, Trump was uttering his familiar lines about the threat posed by illegal immigrants and other perceived threats to the US. As his campaign continued, it attracted unusual figures like Elon Musk and Robert F. Kennedy Jr., supplying a certain color to the elections.

Trump also replaced Mike Pence as vice president with J. D. Vance, a Scots-Irish US Senator from Ohio who had authored a memoir, *Hillbilly Elegy*, about growing up in Appalachia and the struggles of the people there. He firmly identified with the Scots-Irish common people against the so-called "elite," writing, "I may be white, but I do not identify with the WASPs of the Northeast. Instead, I identify with the millions of working-class white Americans of Scots-Irish descent who have no college degree...Americans call them hillbillies, rednecks, or white trash. I call them neighbors, friends, and family."[282] For Vance, Trump and his MAGA movement were giving voice and speaking to precisely his demographic in challenging the corrupt and oppressive "elite" which ran America's institutions.

As it turned out, the 2024 election was historic in that a sitting president running for reelection, who had triumphed in the primaries, was ousted from the race just weeks before the convention. The reason lay in Biden and Trump's first televised debate in June 2024 in which Biden seemed to fall apart, sounding hoarse and appearing distracted and dazed. Some commentators described Biden's debate performance as the worst in US history.[283] There was already much discussion of Biden's health and vitality, with Republicans describing him as senile and accusing the White House of a conspiracy to cover up his condition.[284] In his eighties and the oldest president in US history, Biden appeared in media images to the American public doddering about, looking absentmindedly, and falling in public, for example, at the Air Force Academy's commencement ceremony in June 2023.

While Biden's allegedly failing health had been a central topic in conservative media for years, Biden's debate performance made it a mainstream concern. Even the suggestion that the president was not fully alert and aware was frightening for many, considering that he

282 J. D. Vance, *Hillbilly Elegy: A Memoir of a Family and Culture in Crisis* (New York: Harper, 2016), p. 3.
283 Jeff Greenfield, "The Worst Debate Performance in American History," *Politico*, June 28, 2024.
284 Ian Ward, "Conservatives See a Conspiracy Around Joe Biden's Stumbles," *Politico*, July 11, 2024.

had his finger on the nuclear button, which could end human life on earth. Every gaffe and verbal slip was now sure to be magnified by the media as Americans wondered if each was an indication of deeper problems and deterioration—for example, Biden, while onstage with President Zelenskyy at the NATO summit in Washington shortly after the debate, referred to him as President Putin.

The Democratic Party now moved against Biden, staging an internal coup to force him out of the race. Biden, convinced that his campaign was untenable, dropped out. He announced, "I've decided the best way forward is to pass the torch to a new generation. That's the best way to unite our nation."[285] "We have to decide," Biden said, "Do we still believe in honesty, decency, and respect; freedom, justice, and democracy?" The Party coalesced behind Kamala Harris, who, although virtually unknown to the American public despite holding high office, made a considerable impact on the electorate. Having secured the firm backing of the Obamas, she hit the ground running, and her ascent to the highest levels of American public life was dramatic. For a few weeks, she seemed to have conquered the media. She attracted huge crowds, invited top celebrities to join her on stage, including Oprah Winfrey, and raised $1 billion to battle Trump. When Harris debated Trump, she seemed to triumph over him. Republican luminaries like former Vice President Dick Cheney also joined in support of Harris, with Cheney declaring, "In our nation's 248-year history, there has never been an individual who is a greater threat to our republic than Donald Trump. He tried to steal the last election using lies and violence to keep himself in power after the voters had rejected him. He can never be trusted with power again."[286] Cheney's

285 "READ: President Biden's Speech on Withdrawing From the 2024 Presidential Race," *U.S. News and World Report*, July 25, 2024: https://www.usnews.com/news/national-news/articles/2024-07-25/read-president-bidens-speech-withdrawing-from-the-2024-presidential-race

286 Juliana Kim, "Dick Cheney says he will vote for Harris," *NPR*, September 7, 2024.

daughter Liz, a former congresswoman, appeared at campaign events with Harris. A number of Trump's own officials, including his White House press secretary, also endorsed Harris.

In the reconstituted presidential race, Trump's anti-immigrant rhetoric escalated even further; for example, he warned that migrants were eating the pets of Americans and of "young American girls being raped and sodomized and murdered by savage criminal aliens."[287] "They will walk into your kitchen, they'll cut your throat," Trump said.[288] He asserted, "The United States is now an occupied country," but promised that his election would bring "liberation" from the immigrants.[289] Trump also made the economic argument that "All of our jobs are being taken by the migrants."[290] He additionally pledged to deploy the National Guard against what he called "the enemy from within."[291] A poll released in October 2024 found that one-third of Americans agreed specifically with Trump's claim that illegal immigrants are "poisoning the blood of our country,"[292] while another released the same month found that nearly half of Americans "support rounding up undocumented immigrants and putting them into militarized camps."[293] Harris, for her part, adopted the slogan

287 Josh Sweigart and Jessica Orozco, "Trump vows to do mass deportations in Springfield, repeats false Haitian claims," *Dayton Daily News*, September 14, 2024.
288 "Trump launches into 'dark speech' on illegal immigration," *AFP*, September 28, 2024.
289 Carolyn Thompson, Jeff Amy, and Calvin Woodward, "Harris and Trump say America tanks if they lose. So why the exuberance at their rallies?," *Associated Press*, October 17, 2024.
290 Victoria Bekiempis, "Harris and Trump tour key swing states as end of campaign draws close," *The Guardian*, November 2, 2024.
291 Stephen Groves, "Trump suggests he'll use the military on 'the enemy from within' the US if he's reelected," *Associated Press*, October 13, 2024.
292 Michael Sainato, "A third of Americans agree with Trump that immigrants 'poison the blood' of US," *The Guardian*, October 18, 2024.
293 "Americans split on idea of putting immigrants in militarized 'camps,'" *Axios*, October 22, 2024.

"We're not going back," a reference to the Trump presidential years and his nostalgia-infused messaging.

In the end, despite fears of chaos, the US held its election on schedule without a fuss or violence. Although the pundits predicted a whisker-thin margin between Trump and Kamala, Americans voted resoundingly for Trump. Not only did he win all seven "swing states," but he also won the popular vote. For only the second time in US history, following President Grover Cleveland in the late nineteenth century, a president was elected to two non-consecutive terms. The election was greeted with shock and despair among those Americans who opposed Trump and Trumpism as it indicated that Trump's support was expanding from his longstanding group of core supporters, not contracting. Republicans also secured majorities in the House and Senate. The Supreme Court was already sympathetic, and now all three arms of government were aligned in Trump's favor. His supporters were elated, and his critics nervous, considering his dark threats of retribution. The cherished principle of checks and balances, the essence of American democracy, was in danger of being upended.

In the election, Trump improved drastically on his previous totals in traditionally Democratic areas and among groups predicted to support Democrats, including Latinos, African Americans, and the young. Trump won the votes of men ages 18 to 29, for example, by 14 points over Harris.[294] Trump also received one out of every three non-white votes that were cast in the election.[295] Even Muslims, deeply agitated as the slaughter continued in Gaza, voted for Trump in large numbers. According to a CAIR exit poll, Trump actually did slightly better among Muslims than Harris, with the lion's share

---

294 Catherine Rampell, "Why Gen Z men love Trump's reign of destruction," *The Washington Post*, February 21, 2025.
295 "Exit Polls," *NBC News*, November 5, 2024: https://www.nbcnews.com/politics/2024-elections/exit-polls

of the Muslim vote going to Green Party candidate Jill Stein.[296] In the closing days of the campaign, Trump made conciliatory remarks about Muslims and invited Muslim leaders to join him onstage. This notably contrasted with Harris and the Democrats, who refused to allow a single Muslim to appear on the stage at the Democratic convention, no doubt due to concerns about what they might say about Gaza.

As the election results came in, a debate ensued about how Trump was able to improve his vote totals across so many groups. Inflation and the high cost of living were widely cited as important factors. Still, Trump's higher totals among groups like Latinos and African Americans also indicated that an increasing number of non-whites accepted Trump's messaging that his MAGA and "America First" movement was open to Americans regardless of background. In the closing days of the campaign, US airwaves were dominated by a Trump anti-transgender ad which ran some 30,000 times, including in every swing state, particularly during football games. Commentators also cited the fact that Harris' recruitment of celebrities may have backfired. There was clearly celebrity fatigue among the public and a mood against established sources of authority and influence. Analysts additionally pointed to Trump's success at reaching out to and mobilizing the so-called "manosphere," a "loosely connected network of online groups" associated with figures like Andrew Tate who agree broadly that masculinity is threatened and in crisis, brought about by a combination of "feminism, leftwing politics, immigration, 'wokeness,'" and other factors.[297] In the aftermath of Trump's victory, the

---

296 Ismail Allison, "CAIR Exit Poll of Muslim Voters Reveals Surge in Support for Jill Stein and Donald Trump, Steep Decline for Harris," CAIR, November 8, 2024: https://www.cair.com/press_releases/cair-exit-poll-of-muslim-voters-reveals-surge-in-support-for-jill-stein-and-donald-trump-steep-decline-for-harris/

297 Steve Rose, "The sad, stupid rise of the sigma male: how toxic masculinity took over social media," *The Guardian*, June 12, 2024; Christine Fernando,

1960s women's rights slogan, "My body, my choice" was reappropriated as "Your body, my choice" and deployed against women online and in schools.[298] A post by the aforementioned Nick Fuentes using the slogan received over 100 million views on "X," the renamed Twitter.com.

Biden, to whom many Americans looked to restore a sense of normalcy, decorum, and compassion in government, seemed to fade from public life after dropping out of the presidential race. In December 2024, he announced that he was pardoning his son Hunter, a longtime target of Republicans. Hunter had been found guilty in federal court of "illegally buying and possessing a gun as a drug user" and neglecting to pay $1.4 million in taxes "while spending lavishly on escorts, strippers, cars and drugs."[299] This was after Biden had stated several times that he would never show any favoritism to his family. On TV, he had repeatedly affirmed, "No one is above the law." The decision caused outrage among many Americans, including members of Biden's own Party. Congressman Greg Landsman, a Democrat from Ohio, said, "as someone who wants people to believe in public service again, it's a setback," while Senator Michael Bennet, a Democrat from Colorado, said Biden's pardon placed "personal interest ahead of duty and further erodes Americans' faith that the justice system is fair and equal for all."[300] In fact, in his statement announcing the pardon, Biden had claimed that it was not, affirming, "I have watched my son being selectively, and unfairly, prosecuted. Without

---

"Emboldened 'manosphere' accelerates threats and demeaning language toward women after US election," *Associated Press*, November 30, 2024.
298 Christine Fernando, "Emboldened 'manosphere' accelerates threats and demeaning language toward women after US election," *Associated Press*, November 30, 2024.
299 MJ Lee, Paula Reid, and Michael Williams, "Democrats left fuming over Biden's decision to pardon his son—after he repeatedly said he wouldn't," *CNN*, December 3, 2024.
300 Ibid.

aggravating factors like use in a crime, multiple purchases, or buying a weapon as a straw purchaser, people are almost never brought to trial on felony charges solely for how they filled out a gun form…I believe in the justice system, but as I have wrestled with this, I also believe raw politics has infected this process and it led to a miscarriage of justice."[301] This description of the judicial system contradicted Biden's stated mission in office to reinforce American institutions and reassure Americans that they were functioning well. Additionally, Biden's own Department of Justice had investigated Hunter Biden. If Biden's assessment was correct, it was an admission that his mission had not been successful, leaving Americans in an even greater state of uncertainty because both Democrat and Republican leaders were now stating that politics had infected the judicial system—Trump had already made what he called the "weaponization" of the judicial system by Biden a cornerstone of his campaign.

There was also talk of taking Biden to court for complicity in war crimes as Israel deployed the deadliest weapons which slaughtered women and children in Gaza. In December 2024, Palestinian families sued Biden's State Department in the US District Court for the District of Columbia on the charge that Secretary of State Antony Blinken "deliberately circumvented a U.S. human rights law to continue funding and supporting Israeli military units accused of atrocities in Gaza and the Israeli-occupied West Bank."[302] A poll conducted by the *Daily Mail* and the J.L. Partners firm published in December 2024 found that Americans had selected Biden as the "worst president in modern American history."[303] Biden's performance was un-

---

301 "Statement from President Joe Biden," The White House, December 1, 2024: https://www.whitehouse.gov/briefing-room/statements-releases/2024/12/01/statement-from-president-joe-biden-11/
302 Kanishka Singh, "Palestinian families sue State Department over US support for Israeli military," *Reuters*, December 17, 2024.
303 Rob Crilly, "Biden will leave office as the 'worst president' in modern history, according to voters in devastating poll," *Daily Mail*, December 6, 2024.

favorably compared with presidents like Reagan and Obama, who received the highest scores.

With just weeks remaining in his presidency, Biden also took the step of allowing Zelenskyy to use sophisticated American weapons that would strike deep in Russia, thus ratcheting up the tension. This immediately increased the danger of the conflict erupting into a nuclear confrontation, which was already threatened by Putin. In this context the move appeared reckless, particularly because Trump was promising a different though nonspecific Ukraine policy which would immediately end the war—as he claimed, within "24 hours" after taking the oath of office.

In the interregnum between Biden and Trump, law and order seemed to continue to deteriorate. A young man shot a health-care CEO fatally in the back, another was acquitted of murder after placing a man he thought was threatening passengers in the subway in a chokehold and killing him, and a man set a woman on fire as she slept in the subway and then stood over her to fan the flames with his shirt. All this happened in a few days towards the end of 2024 in one city, New York, where the mayor, Eric Adams, had been indicted three months earlier for bribery, conspiracy, wire fraud, and soliciting contributions for his campaign from foreign nationals.[304] On the first day of 2025 there were two attacks by US soldiers, adding to the sense of insecurity. In New Orleans, an Army veteran and American convert to Islam claiming allegiance to ISIS rammed his car into the crowd of revelers on Bourbon Street, killing 14 people before being shot by police, while in Las Vegas an active-duty Green Beret blew himself up, seemingly in desperation, complaining of weak American leaders and warning that the US was heading for collapse.

Meanwhile, Trump was busy issuing his nominations for top posts in his new administration, which led to an immediate backlash

---

304 Eric Levenson and Celina Tebor, "What's in the 5-count indictment against NYC Mayor Eric Adams," *CNN*, September 26, 2024.

from those who protested that the nominees were unqualified—his Secretary of Defense, Pete Hegseth, for example, was a Fox News host with no senior leadership or management experience who was observed chanting "Kill all Muslims!" in a bar.[305] Matt Gaetz resigned from the House as Trump nominated him for the post of Attorney General. A storm of controversy followed, and scandalous stories of sex and depravity circulated. Inevitably, Gaetz fell. In the meantime, the appointment to senior positions of figures from Trump's first term, such as Stephen Miller and Sebastian Gorka, created fear among minorities and immigrants.

Other Trump nominees included Darren Beattie as Under Secretary for Public Diplomacy at the State Department, who wrote that Trump referring to "Shithole countries" was the "high-point" of his presidency and stated, "Competent white men must be in charge if you want things to work. Unfortunately, our entire national ideology is predicated on coddling the feelings of women and minorities, and demoralizing competent white men."[306] Howard Lutnick, Trump's Secretary of Commerce, who lost 658 of his investment bank employees at the World Trade Center on 9/11 including his brother, urged Americans to vote for Trump in 2024 "because we must crush Jihad."[307]

While in his moment of triumph, Trump nominated some standard right-wing politicians in his government, there were also encouraging signs of minority appointments such as Senator Marco

305 Casey Tolan, Curt Devine, Rob Kuznia, and Brian Stelter, "As Hegseth's public profile grew, he faced deepening private turmoil," *CNN*, December 5, 2024.
306 Andrew Kaczynski, Jennifer Hansler, and Em Steck, "Trump appoints speechwriter fired for attending conference with White nationalists to top State Department role," *CNN*, February 3, 2025.
307 Swapna Venugopal Ramaswamy and Michael Collins, "Howard Lutnick, Trump's transition co-chair, is his pick to lead Commerce Department," *USA Today*, November 19, 2024.

Rubio, Trump's choice for Secretary of State. Rubio became the first Latino in US history to serve in that position. Trump also selected Dr. Mehmet Oz, the Muslim heart surgeon and television host, to oversee the US Centers for Medicare and Medicaid Services, which administers both healthcare programs. Trump additionally appointed the distinguished Islamic scholar Hamza Yusuf and Ismail Royer to advise his newly established White House Religious Liberty Commission. Then there was Robert F. Kennedy Jr., son of the American pluralist icon, who began running for president as an independent before joining Trump's campaign. Trump now named him head of the US Department of Health and Human Services. Kennedy, a famous anti-vaccine activist, had argued that COVID-19 was a bioweapon specifically, as he put it, "targeted to attack Caucasians and black people. The people who are most immune are Ashkenazi Jews and Chinese."[308] Kennedy became the butt of TV comedy show hosts picking on the putative worm in his brain[309] and strange actions, such as admitting to transporting a dead bear to New York's Central Park and dumping it there.[310] As Trump named more picks, there were howls of outrage from the media, especially the left-leaning sections. They pointed to the numerous individuals on the lists accused of sexual assault, corruption, and suffering from alcohol problems. It seemed fortuitous then that the London *Economist* selected kakistocracy or rule of the worst for its 2024 word of the year. Providing a perspective that echoed the *Economist* was the Oxford dictionary word of the year, "brain rot."

It was difficult to relate the current American leaders to the caliber and quality of American leadership of a generation or two ago—

---

308 "Fact-checking RFK Jr's views on health policy," *BBC News*, November 15, 2024.
309 Michelle Shen, "NYT: RFK Jr. says worm 'got into my brain and ate a portion of it,'" *CNN*, May 8, 2024.
310 Emma G. Fitzsimmons, "Robert F. Kennedy Jr. Admits He Left a Dead Bear in Central Park," *The New York Times*, August 4, 2024.

Ronald Reagan, the Kennedys, Martin Luther King Jr., Malcolm X, and scholars like Noam Chomsky, who remains an important moral voice. Before them, there were giants like Eisenhower and Franklin D. Roosevelt, and beyond them, Abraham Lincoln and the great Founding Fathers, Washington, Jefferson, and Franklin. The death of President Jimmy Carter in December 2024 at the age of 100 was a reminder of the greatness of a pluralist leader who, with his civility, humility, compassion, and faith, both in and out of the White House, was the nearest thing to a living saint in American leadership.

Trump 2.0: Predator Identity Rampant

The ascendancy of Trump once again to the presidency in 2025 marked a high-water mark for predator identity it had not experienced since at least the immediate post-9/11 era. Trump had broken through the general lack of movement in the three identities which had persisted for the past two decades, as discussed above. This was a president who had issued videos referencing the creation of a "unified Reich" in the USA[311] and had spent much of the election year having the threat of prison hang like Damocles' sword over him following his conviction on 34 counts by a New York court. He of course had already been impeached for "incitement of insurrection" against the United States. And yet, Trump's message on matters such as immigrants poisoning American blood was embraced by a clear majority. As the prominent *The New York Times* columnist Maureen Dowd noted, "Trump is returning as a colossus."[312]

With many among the predator and primordial camps energized, pluralist identity was at a low ebb. With Biden having faltered and Harris convincingly defeated, there were not yet clear leaders assum-

311 Mike Wendling and Jake Horton, "Trump campaign deletes video mentioning 'unified Reich,'" *BBC News*, May 21, 2024.
312 Maureen Dowd, "Trump Brings a Chill to Washington," *The New York Times*, January 18, 2025.

ing the mantle for the future. At a time when pluralist identity needed to be resolute and confident, many of its adherents initially appeared dispirited and divided. While the Founding Fathers gave broad guidance in terms of pluralism—all humans being created equal, religious freedom, freedom of speech and assembly in which differences could be voiced and protected, democracy, and the rule of law—there had already in the past been at least two "re-foundings" of the US, to use a term favored by American historians,[313] which expanded and codified these ideals along pluralist lines. The first was the Civil War and Reconstruction and the second was the Civil Rights Movement and the laws which resulted from it. During fieldwork for *Journey into America*, Jesse Jackson confirmed this idea when I asked him who his favorite Founding Father was and he replied, "Dr. King."

Now, the very definition of aspects of pluralism such as "diversity, equity, and inclusion," intended to create a welcoming environment in the country for all people, were being contested. Did promoting diversity mean ensuring that every institution "look like America" as Biden said about his cabinet? Did institutions themselves have an obligation to voice their support for causes of pluralism and justice as so many companies did in 2020 when they supported Black Lives Matter—or indeed, as intellectuals and activists like Ibram X. Kendi argued, to become "anti-racist"? Was it an imperative additionally to dismantle what Bernie Sanders and Biden called the "oligarchy"? In Biden's farewell address, he referenced Eisenhower's warning about the "military industrial complex" to warn of the "dangerous concentration of power in the hands of very few ultra-wealthy people… an oligarchy is taking shape in America of extreme wealth, power,

---

313 Eric Foner, *The Second Founding: How the Civil War and Reconstruction Remade the Constitution* (New York: W. W. Norton & Company, 2019); David W. Blight, "In Memory's Mirror," *The American Interest*, Vol. 7, No. 1, September 1, 2011.

and influence that literally threatens our entire democracy, our basic rights and freedoms, and a fair shot for everyone to get ahead."[314]

There was also the question of how long the affirmative action policies instituted nationwide in the 1960s, which focused on increasing opportunities for and hiring women and people from non-white minority groups, would need to remain in effect. "Affirmative action" policies, a term first used by John F. Kennedy,[315] were upheld by the Supreme Court, for example, in 2003, on the expectation that they were "temporary" and "25 years from now, the use of racial preferences will no longer be necessary to [achieve diversity]."[316] In 2023, the Supreme Court decided that affirmative action had run its course, and determined it to be unconstitutional. Like the previous years' Supreme Court decision to overturn *Roe vs. Wade* and remove the federal right to abortion for women which was in place for nearly five decades, the affirmative action decision was an upending of social and legal norms that many Americans had believed were settled.

Both decisions, however, were celebrated by Trump, who held them up as great victories. As president once again he moved to go even further in challenging and dismantling the United States that had taken shape in the aftermath of the Civil Rights Movement and even before—he sought nothing less than the overturning and transformation of the post-Second World War America and the global system that it established and led.

---

314 "Remarks by President Biden in a Farewell Address to the Nation," The White House, January 15, 2025: https://bidenwhitehouse.archives.gov/briefing-room/speeches-remarks/2025/01/15/remarks-by-president-biden-in-a-farewell-address-to-the-nation/
315 Jackie Mansky, "The History Behind the Supreme Court's Affirmative Action Decision," *Smithsonian Magazine*, June 29, 2023.
316 Richard Lempert, "The Supreme Court is poised to reverse affirmative action: Here's what you need to know," The Brookings Institution, June 5, 2023: https://www.brookings.edu/articles/the-supreme-court-is-poised-to-reverse-affirmative-action-heres-what-you-need-to-know/

Within hours of assuming the presidency in 2025, Trump began issuing dozens of executive orders with unprecedented rapidity. He declared an end to "birthright citizenship," pardoned all the January 6 rioters, including violent offenders, suspended all refugee admissions, mandated that there were two sexes, male and female, and abolished all "Diversity, Equity, and Inclusion" (DEI) programs in the federal government. Trump also revoked President Lyndon B. Johnson's 1965 executive order mandating "equal opportunity" in federal hiring and training practices and removed a ban on federal contractors allowing "segregated facilities" such as drinking fountains.[317] Anything that could be considered "DEI" was removed across the federal government. The policy resulted in notable actions such as the Pentagon website marking for deletion mentions of the *Enola Gay* plane which dropped the atom bomb on Japan because it included the word "gay"[318] and the US Naval Academy removing the prominent Black American author Maya Angelou's *I Know Why the Caged Bird Sings* from its library but leaving Hitler's *Mein Kampf*.[319] Commentators noted that Trump's actions were part of the continuing backlash to the events of 2020 involving Black Lives Matter and included nothing less than "a systematic effort to unravel Lyndon B. Johnson's civil rights legacy, rolling back protections that have shaped American life for nearly six decades."[320]

Trump additionally took a wrecking ball through the federal government bureaucracy, empowering Elon Musk and his Department

317 Kanishka Singh, "Trump administration removes ban on 'segregated facilities' in federal contracts," *Reuters*, March 19, 2025.
318 Tara Copp, Lolita C. Baldor, and Kevin Vineys, "War heroes and military firsts are among 26,000 images flagged for removal in Pentagon's DEI purge," *Associated Press*, March 7, 2025.
319 John Ismay, "Who's In and Who's Out at the Naval Academy's Library?," *The New York Times*, April 11, 2025.
320 Russell Contreras, "Trump's 2025 seeks to reverse LBJ's 1965," *Axios*, March 22, 2025.

of Government Efficiency (DOGE) to eliminate thousands of jobs and even entire agencies—recall Bannon's vow to deconstruct "the administrative state" which was believed to be a bastion of the subversive, corrupt, and anti-American "establishment." With lightning-fast speed, agencies like the US Agency for International Development (USAID), which was created by President Kennedy and provided assistance to the poorest people in the world, were abolished.

In the case of USAID, the sudden suspension of its operations was described as a "death sentence for millions of people"[321] by the UN's World Food Program. A few months later, the White House proposed "eliminating funding for nearly all international organizations, including the United Nations, many of its agencies and for NATO headquarters."[322] Trump had already dismantled US diplomatic media outlets such as the Voice of America, Radio Free Europe, and Radio Free Asia—the White House accused the Voice of America, for example, of being "radical propaganda," "leftist," and "anti-Trump."[323]

Organizations that presented a positive face to the rest of the world such as the US Institute of Peace and Wilson Center were also shuttered. Trump explained that such organizations were not in keeping with his "America First" agenda. In major speeches and statements, Trump mocked USAID for funding "diversity and inclusion" programs and sending money to "Gaza to buy condoms for Hamas," despite there being no evidence this had actually oc-

---

321 Ellen Knickmeyer, Samy Magdy, and David Biller, "The US ends lifesaving food aid for millions. The World Food Program calls it a 'death sentence,'" *Associated Press*, April 8, 2025.
322 Matthew Lee and Farnoush Amiri, "White House proposes drastic cuts to State Department and funding for UN, NATO and other groups," *Associated Press*, April 14, 2025.
323 "The Voice of Radical America," The White House, March 15, 2025: https://www.whitehouse.gov/articles/2025/03/the-voice-of-radical-america/

curred.[324] Trump also ridiculed US aid to countries like Lesotho, remarking in a speech to Congress, "Eight million dollars to promote LGBTQI+ in the African nation of Lesotho, which nobody has ever heard of."[325] Three months into Trump's term, some 200,000 US federal workers from multiple agencies had been sacked.[326]

The manner in which the firings were conducted itself made a statement. It was not done in a normal bureaucratic way but rapidly, without warning, and with secrecy. It exhibited a cruelty both towards the employees who overnight found themselves without jobs and the people benefitting from their work, for example the recipients of American aid. The rationale lay in the designation of the federal workers by Trump and his administration as the "enemy" making up the "deep state." As is often the case against an enemy, no quarter was given. That federal workers played essential roles in the running of the country and had immense knowledge, expertise, and experience in their own fields did not matter.

Another target was the jewel in America's crown, its system of universities. While the nation's universities were the envy of the world, like the federal government, they were seen by Trump and his followers as part of the "establishment" and targeted along the lines of predator identity. As J. D. Vance stated, "the universities are the enemy" and "we have to honestly and aggressively attack the universities in this country."[327] Vance also, for good measure, cited

---

324 Melissa Goldin, "FACT FOCUS: No evidence that $50 million was designated by the US to buy condoms for Hamas," *Associated Press*, January 29, 2025.
325 Nellie Peyton, "Lesotho insulted after Trump says nobody has heard of the country," *Reuters*, March 6, 2025.
326 "How hard have Trump and Musk layoffs hit US agencies?," *Reuters*, April 1, 2025.
327 Irie Sentner, "Republicans have hated universities for years. Anti-war protests gave them a reason to punish them," *Politico*, March 11, 2025.

President Richard Nixon, who said, "The press is the enemy. The establishment is the enemy. The professors are the enemy."[328]

Trump used the power of the purse, freezing billions of dollars of federal research funding to multiple universities unless they acquiesced to his demands, for example abolishing DEI programs and cracking down on pro-Palestine activism. In an unprecedented action, Trump ordered private universities to remove the leadership of academic departments. At Columbia University, the epicenter of the pro-Palestine protests, the university yielded to Trump's demand to replace the head of the Middle Eastern, South Asian, and African Studies Department, announcing it would instead be run by a senior vice provost under an "academic receivership" arrangement.[329] Trump assailed universities such as Harvard for pushing what he called "political, ideological, and terrorist inspired/supporting 'Sickness.'"[330] Prominent professors including Jason Stanley at Yale University announced they were fleeing the US for Canada, with Stanley stating, "ultimately, it is like leaving Germany in 1932, 33, 34. There's resonance: my grandmother left Berlin with my father in 1939. So it's a family tradition."[331] Commentators such as Fareed Zakaria warned that Trump's actions concerning education resembled China's Cultural Revolution, "when an increasingly paranoid

---

328 "175. Conversation Among President Nixon, the President's Assistant for National Security Affairs (Kissinger), and the President's Deputy Assistant for National Security Affairs (Haig)," Department of State, Office of the Historian, December 14, 1972: https://history.state.gov/historicaldocuments/frus1969-76v09/d175; Gretchen McNamara, "Professors are not the enemy. Issue 1 will stop agenda pushed by JD Vance, GOP lawmakers," *The Columbus Dispatch*, September 11, 2024.

329 Troy Closson, "Columbia Makes Concessions to Trump Amid Bid to Reclaim Federal Funds," *The New York Times*, March 21, 2025.

330 Brandon Drenon, "Trump threatens Harvard's tax-exempt status after freezing $2bn funding," *BBC News*, April 16, 2025.

331 Rachel Leingang, "Yale professor who studies fascism fleeing US to work in Canada," *The Guardian*, March 26, 2025.

Mao Zedong smashed China's established universities, a madness that took generations to remedy."[332]

Trump set to work enacting the "largest domestic deportation operation in American history" which he promised during the campaign. In his speech to a joint session of Congress in March 2025 he claimed progress, stating, "we are achieving the great liberation of America" from "the migrant occupation."[333] Early in his term he began sending deportees to the prison at Guantanamo Bay and ordered the Navy to prepare for an influx of 30,000,[334] before the emphasis shifted to El Salvador's Terrorism Confinement Center. Not only is the Terrorism Confinement Center the largest prison in Latin America, but it is also the largest prison in the world.[335] Trump announced with great fanfare deals with the El Salvadoran president, Nayib Bukele, who called himself "the world's coolest dictator," to accept deported American migrants including from countries such as Venezuela. Trump even said that he wanted to send US citizens to El Salvador to be incarcerated.[336] Todd Lyons, the director of DHS' Immigration and Customs Enforcement (ICE) agency, spoke clinically about the lives of the people involved, saying of the deportations, "We need to get better at treating this like

---

332 Fareed Zakaria, "Trump is launching America's version of the Cultural Revolution," *The Washington Post*, March 14, 2025.

333 "Remarks by President Trump in Joint Address to Congress," The White House, March 4, 2025: https://www.whitehouse.gov/remarks/2025/03/remarks-by-president-trump-in-joint-address-to-congress/

334 Carol Rosenberg, "How Guantánamo Bay Figures in the Trump Immigration Crackdown," *The New York Times*, April 4, 2025.

335 Vera Bergengruen and Michelle Hackman, "El Salvador's Bukele Plans to Double the Size of Giant Prison Holding U.S. Deportees," *The Wall Street Journal*, April 16, 2025.

336 Nicholas Riccardi, "Trump says he wants to imprison US citizens in El Salvador. That's likely illegal," *Associated Press*, April 15, 2025.

a business" and that the process should be "like [Amazon] Prime, but with human beings."[337]

The effect on the communities involved was immediate. Yakie Palma, a second-grade teacher of Salvadoran background in Prince George's County, Maryland, where a large number of Central American migrants reside, told CNN that "her students' Salvadoran parents are now terrified to do everyday tasks like pick up their children from school. The young students are also anxious, depressed and sleep deprived, which is impacting their performance on exams and assignments."[338] Members of the community like Kilmar Armando Abrego Garcia, a sheet-metal laborer blamed for being part of the MS-13 gang, were seized and flown to El Salvador for imprisonment in the Terrorism Confinement Center. While the Trump administration admitted it had made a mistake in deporting Garcia—whose young autistic son was reduced to seeking out his father's work shirts to smell in order to feel close to him[339]—it still had not perceptibly facilitated Garcia's return, as ordered by the US Supreme Court.

In a similar case, when a federal judge ordered two planes bound for El Salvador full of Venezuelans being deported for purported membership in the gang Tren de Aragua to turn back, the Trump administration ignored the judge, and the prisoners were incarcerated in the Terrorism Confinement Center. Trump, in accordance with his view that migrants were "invaders," had invoked the 1798 Alien Enemies Act, which was used to incarcerate the Japanese during the Second World War, arguing that it allowed him wide latitude to immediately deport "enemy aliens." *The New York*

337 Marina Dunbar, "Ice director wants to run deportations like 'Amazon Prime for human beings,'" *The Guardian*, April 9, 2025.
338 Polo Sandoval, Linh Tran, Dalia Faheid, Alaa Elassar, and Priscilla Alvarez, "After a Maryland father was mistakenly deported, his community prepares for the worst," *CNN*, April 4, 2025.
339 Ibid.

Times, which looked into the over 200 Venezuelans on the flights, found that "most of the men do not have criminal records in the United States or elsewhere in the region, beyond immigration offenses" and "very few of them appear to have any clear, documented links to the Venezuelan gang."[340]

The administration's attitude to such legal rulings which went against their policies was summed up by Vance, who, referencing President Andrew Jackson's reported reaction to the Supreme Court during the Cherokee "Trail of Tears," stated, "when the courts stop you, stand before the country like Andrew Jackson did and say: 'The chief justice has made his ruling. Now let him enforce it.'"[341] The reaction set up a direct clash between the executive and judicial branch expected to persist into Trump's term; *The Atlantic* declared, "The Constitutional Crisis Is Here."[342] For Vance, in keeping with predator identity, the stakes were too high to allow judges to influence the Trump administration's policies because the existence and future of the nation itself was believed to be at stake. Regarding immigrants, for example, Vance invoked his Scots-Irish forebearers in condemning what he called a "mass invasion of the country my ancestors built with their bare hands."[343]

Concerning Muslims and Islam, Trump, who promised to reinstate the "Muslim ban," issued an executive order the day he began his second term titled "Protecting the United States from Foreign Terrorists and Other National Security and Public Safety Threats," which required the government to provide a list of countries for

---

340 Julie Turkewitz, Jazmine Ulloa, Isayen Herrera, Hamed Aleaziz, and Zolan Kanno-Youngs, "'Alien Enemies' or Innocent Men? Inside Trump's Rushed Effort to Deport 238 Migrants," *The New York Times*, April 15, 2025.
341 Ian Ward, "There's No Need to Guess. JD Vance Is Ready to Ignore the Courts," *Politico*, February 11, 2025.
342 Adam Serwer, "The Constitutional Crisis Is Here," *The Atlantic*, April 14, 2025.
343 J. D. Vance, X.com, April 16, 2025.

which "partial or full suspension on the admission of nationals" may be imposed. Weeks later, Trump's director of national intelligence, Tulsi Gabbard, declared "radical Islamist terrorism" to be the greatest threat to the US.[344]

One by one, Muslims and others on student visas in the US were seized off the streets by security agents and sent to US prisons to await deportations. Every day, student visas were being revoked, with the number reaching at least 800 three months into Trump's term.[345] Secretary of State Marco Rubio said that "a lot" of the people so affected had participated in pro-Palestine protests.[346] The students and those on other kinds of visas were being ordered expelled under a 1950s Cold War-era law which gives the secretary of state broad authority to expel foreign citizens deemed to pose "potentially serious adverse foreign policy consequences" for the US.

The first major case to be announced was that of Mahmoud Khalil, a Palestinian refugee born in Syria who had been a student at Columbia participating in the protests and was now living legally in the US with his pregnant 28-year-old Syrian American wife. Trump said that the arrest of Khalil, who was flown from New York to a prison in Louisiana, was the "first arrest of many to come," and he accused Khalil of "anti-American activity."[347] Trump vowed, "We will find, apprehend, and deport these terrorist sympathizers from our country—never to return again. If you support terrorism, including the slaughtering of innocent men, women, and children,

---

344 Corey Walker, "US Intel Chief Tulsi Gabbard Declares 'Radical Islamist Terrorism' Most Urgent National Security Threat," *The Algemeiner*, February 25, 2025.
345 Kate Selig, "What We Know About the Detentions of Student Protesters," *The New York Times*, March 27, 2025.
346 Ibid.
347 Anna Betts, "Trump calls arrest of Palestinian activist Mahmoud Khalil 'first of many to come,'" *The Guardian*, March 10, 2025.

your presence is contrary to our national and foreign policy interests, and you are not welcome here."[348]

Khalil's wife, Noor Abdalla, a dentist born and raised in Michigan who wears the hijab, denied that her husband was pro-Hamas and said of the day Khalil was taken in the middle of the night from their house, "I don't think I've ever experienced anything scarier."[349] And yet, she felt it was characteristic of the Islamophobia she had grown up with after 9/11: "It kind of brought back a lot of things that I experienced growing up in the United States. In New York the other day, me and my husband were walking and someone said, like, called me a terrorist. So, it's like constantly throughout my whole life. I think most Muslims in this country can relate to that. It doesn't matter what I say; that's what they think of me, and that's what they're going to think of me."[350]

Videos circulated of other cases, such as Rumeysa Ozturk, a Turkish graduate student at Tufts University, who was seen being arrested by plainclothes officers while on her way to break the Ramadan fast with friends—the government said that Ozturk had "engaged in activities in support of Hamas, a foreign terrorist organization that relishes the killing of Americans."[351] To determine targets for removal, government investigators searched "videos, online posts and news clippings of campus protests against the Israel-Hamas war."[352] The Council on American-Islamic Relations (CAIR) warned all Muslims, even US citizens, that while leaving or entering the US they might have their phones taken and data

348 Ibid.
349 Erin Moriarty, "Noor Abdalla on the arrest of her husband, Mahmoud Khalil: 'I was terrified,'" *CBS News*, March 23, 2025.
350 Ibid.
351 Kate Selig, "What We Know About the Detentions of Student Protesters," *The New York Times*, March 27, 2025.
352 Ibid.

downloaded by US authorities.[353] CAIR wasn't the only ones, however. Even the European Union began issuing officials with burner phones when visiting the US because doing so was now seen as a potential security risk.[354]

For the US counterterrorism director, Sebastian Gorka, those who opposed Trump's goals and policies of deporting millions were themselves implicated in terrorism. Framing and articulating predator identity clearly, he stated, "There's one line that divides us: Do you love America, or do you hate America? It's really quite that simple...We have people who love America, like the president, like his cabinet, like the directors of his agencies, who want to protect Americans. And then there is the other side that is on the side of the cartel members, on the side of the illegal aliens, on the side of the terrorists—and you have to ask yourself: Are they technically aiding and abetting them? Because aiding and abetting criminals and terrorists is a crime."[355]

Concerning Muslims abroad, Trump, after playing an important role in securing a temporary Gaza ceasefire and releasing some of the hostages held by Hamas, announced his plan for the US to "take," "own," and "clean out" Gaza. This would entail expelling its two million Palestinians, in order to build what Trump described as the "Riviera of the Middle East."[356] Trump also began bombing what he called "Houthi barbarians"[357] in Yemen follow-

353 Nick Mordowanec, "U.S. Citizens May Have Phones Searched After Traveling, CAIR Warns," *Newsweek*, April 2, 2025.
354 Andy Bounds, "EU issues US-bound staff with burner phones over spying fears," *Financial Times*, April 14, 2025.
355 Jim Thomas, "Gorka to Newsmax: '3 Strikes and You're Out' for Abrego Garcia," *Newsmax*, April 15, 2025.
356 Paul Adams, "Why does Trump want to take over Gaza and could he do it?," *BBC News*, February 11, 2025.
357 Jon Gambrell, "Trump threatens Houthi rebels that they'll be 'completely annihilated' as airstrikes pound Yemen," *Associated Press*, March 20, 2025.

ing Houthi attacks on ships in the Red Sea, and told Iran that if they did not make a deal with the US over their nuclear program, "There will be bombing, and it will be bombing the likes of which they have never seen before."[358] Trump also bombed ISIS targets in Somalia, vowing, "WE WILL FIND YOU, AND WE WILL KILL YOU!"[359] and announced further strikes against an ISIS leader in Iraq: "His miserable life was terminated...PEACE THROUGH STRENGTH!"[360]

Concerning Ukraine, as negotiations dragged on, Trump placed considerable blame on Zelenskyy for not being serious about making a "deal." Trump's February 2025 Oval Office meeting with Zelenskyy rapidly deteriorated into a shouting match, with Trump telling Zelenskyy, "you are gambling with World War Three" and Vance calling Zelenskyy "disrespectful." An international outcry followed, with CNN stating, "never before has an American president verbally attacked his visitor like Trump did to Zelenskyy"[361] and *The Washington Post* comparing Trump to a mafia boss.[362]

With US support for NATO and Ukraine up in the air and Trump demanding control of Ukrainian minerals as well as a crucial Ukrainian natural gas pipeline,[363] European leaders, who had

---

358 Nayera Abdallah, "Iran says it will give US talks about nuclear plans a 'genuine chance,'" *Reuters*, April 11, 2025.

359 Mary Harper, "Why Trump is on the warpath in Somalia," *BBC News*, February 6, 2025.

360 Mary Kay Mallonee and Edward Szekeres, "US and Iraqi forces kill ISIS chief of global operations, officials say," *CNN*, March 15, 2025.

361 Kevin Liptak, Jeff Zeleny, Kaitlan Collins, and Kit Maher, "Trump and Vance erupt at Zelensky in tense Oval Office meeting," *CNN*, February 28, 2025.

362 "In acrimonious meeting, Trump berates Zelensky," *The Washington Post*, February 28, 2025.

363 Matthew Luxmoore, "Ukraine's Zelensky Wants Better Terms on Minerals Deal Demanded by Trump," *The Wall Street Journal*, February 23, 2025; Luke Harding, "US 'demands control' from Ukraine of key pipeline

hoped Trump's bark would be worse than his bite on these and other issues, now prepared for an entirely new relationship with the US.

This was particularly the case after Trump, in an act which appeared even to many of his supporters as irresponsible and irrational, imposed tariffs on goods from all countries entering the US including Europe, because, he said, the US was being "ripped off"; an EU official told the *Financial Times*, "The transatlantic alliance is over."[364] With China it became a game of chicken and a global standoff ensued as to who would blink first while both countries kept pushing the tariff totals higher and higher. Foreign leaders were plunged into anxiety and curiosity about how Trump's policies would affect their nations. Economists such as Paul Krugman stated that Trump was effectively bringing about the end of globalization itself.[365]

Trump furthermore announced plans to annex large territories to the US. He said that Canada should be incorporated to become the 51st state, and he took to referring to Prime Minister Justin Trudeau as "governor." He stated that the US would now "take back" the Panama Canal, the building of which was initiated by President Theodore Roosevelt, or else "something very powerful is going to happen."[366] Trump additionally vowed to annex Greenland, the world's largest island, "one way or another" from Danish rule, and refused to rule out the use of force.[367] As Vice President

---

carrying Russian gas," *The Guardian*, April 12, 2025.

364 Andy Bounds, "EU issues US-bound staff with burner phones to avoid espionage," *Financial Times*, April 14, 2025.

365 Scott Tong and Julia Corcoran, "Economist Paul Krugman on globalization and tariffs," *WBUR*, April 8, 2025.

366 Samantha Waldenberg and Michael Rios, "Trump reiterates threat to retake Panama Canal 'or something very powerful' will happen," *CNN*, February 2, 2025.

367 Jon Wertheim, "Why Trump wants Greenland, and what people who call

Vance arrived in Greenland in March 2025 with a message that the US would offer better protection than Denmark had, the Fox News host Jesse Watters declared proudly, "Manifest Destiny is back."[368] Not only Americans, but the inhabitants of these countries and the entire world watched with goggle-eyed fascination and high anxiety as predator identity played havoc on the world stage.

Having triumphed against all odds, Trump was indeed reigning supreme. His cabinet meetings shown on television exhibited a sycophancy which would put the Oriental Shahs of Persia to shame as each member strove to outdo the other in praise of the leader. Trump also had his eye on the future, announcing early his desire to run for a third presidential term, which was not only against the tradition set by George Washington of limiting oneself to two terms, but was banned by the US Constitution. Trump's allies were nevertheless bullish on the prospect, with Steve Bannon stating in April 2025 that the ban and the Constitution itself "is open for interpretation."[369] Bannon vowed, "President Trump is going to run for a third term, and President Trump is going to be elected again on the afternoon of January 20th of 2029. He's going to be President of the United States."[370]

Political commentators were as baffled and uncertain about future trends as was the electorate and politicians themselves. They also expressed fear. Republican Senators such as Lisa Murkowski of Alaska, who had publicly challenged Trump, for example on his treatment of Zelenskyy and alignment with Putin, admitted, "We are all afraid" of retaliation by the Trump administration: "We're in a time and place where—I don't know, I certainly have not—I have

the world's largest island home have to say about it," *60 Minutes*, CBS News, April 13, 2025.
368 *Jesse Watters Primetime*, Fox News, March 28, 2025.
369 Alex Galbraith, "'He's going to have a third term': Bannon tells Maher Trump is sticking around in 2028," *Salon*, April 13, 2025.
370 Ibid.

not been here before. And I'll tell you, I'm oftentimes very anxious myself about using my voice because retaliation is real. And that's not right."[371] Meanwhile, the rest of the world held its breath as it wondered what direction the US would take.

---

371 Giselle Ruhiyyih Ewing, "'We are all afraid': Murkowski says fear of retaliation from Trump administration is 'real,'" *Politico*, April 17, 2025.

Conclusion The Importance of the American Vision

The pendulum that swung toward predator identity reached an extreme point on January 6, 2021. Following this unprecedented event, there was talk of Trump imposing martial law. The United States came within a whisker of adopting predator identity in its most undiluted and unadulterated form in response to Biden's electoral victory, which demonstrated the staying power of pluralist identity. And yet, as discussed above concerning Obama's presidency, it is an identity still reeling from the post-9/11 period, which has had lingering effects. Trump's reelection has concurrently demonstrated the staying power of predator identity with its base in primordial identity. Trump's triumph set predator identity up for potential long-term dominance, both at home and abroad.

At the same time, it is important to keep in mind that even with Trump's victory over Harris in the popular vote, at 50 percent to 48 percent, the identities continue to be roughly balanced one against the other. Pluralist identity remains resilient and deeply rooted, and will be motivated to preserve and promote its understanding of American identity. This balance in the United States contrasts with other nations where predator identity has emerged to dominate the political and cultural landscape, such as Viktor Orbán's

Hungary and Narendra Modi's India. As we have emphasized above, American identities may appear down and out but they return with force—and the pendulum begins to swing in their favor. Even with the first flush of his remarkable victory Trump as president in 2025 was showing interesting signs of pluralist America. He refused to be pushed into a war with Iran, even calling the Iranian people "great," and he hosted an iftar dinner for Muslims in March in which he told the Muslim community they had a friend in the White House who "loved" them.

The strength of America for us is not predator identity, which often can be seen as a tribally influenced desire to protect one's "own" community based on religion, race, or "culture" against perceived "threats," and exists the world over, such as among Europe's far-right. America's pluralist identity makes it unique and links it to the rest of humanity. American pluralist identity should serve as a guide for the nation's leadership, a compass they should follow and always keep in mind.

Revisiting *Journey into America* was a reminder of the unique and long-lasting vision that the Founding Fathers gave the United States and the world—the pluralist identity represented by Jefferson's phrase "all men are created equal" that has consistently proven an inspiration to those seeking human equality in all its forms. Martin Luther King Jr. is only one prominent example in the US. It was also a time to reflect on the nation's past and its future.

Much remained unresolved and uncertain as America contin-ued to grapple with questions of its own identity, its place in the world, its domestic and foreign policies, the place of minorities such as Muslims in its society, and how to address the problems it faced. The immediate dangers facing American leadership are many and on many fronts: the real threat of climate change playing havoc across the continent; the ever-widening gap between the rich and poor; the tensions and conflicts between classes, races, and religions; and above all the hazards of foreign policy, with the emergence of China and Russia as "peer hegemons," to use international relations scholar John Mearsheimer's "realist" frame, and the simmering situation in the Middle East, where, as I write these lines, the Gaza-Israel war continues to take its nightmare and apocalyptic toll in lives and destruction of property. There were also questions about how the US would handle immigration and the fate of the large numbers of undocumented people in the country; the lingering effects of the coronavirus pandemic, which, however ugly and malicious, had illustrated the connectivity of the human race, and deal with any new pandemic that might come; as well as how the US will manage and guide the increasing prominence and development of AI and the changes and challenges that it will pose to American life. Tackling these crises will require constant vigilance, compassion, and intelligence. American leadership will be sorely tested. The nation needed wise and compassionate leadership and direction. Unless strong leadership emerged in young politicians, there was little hope of a satisfactory resolution between the primordial, predator, and pluralist identities that were pulling America apart.

What we could predict was that the contours of our three identities would remain strong. In that, too, it is well to remind ourselves that the representatives of one form of identity may well, at another time in their lives, move to another identity; in short, though his early second term moves were purely in the predator mode, it is possible for a man like Trump to gravitate towards primordial and even pluralist identity—in the way that Biden had appeared to abandon pluralist ideals and adopted a more predatory stance on issues such as immigration and Gaza, or as Obama did in his embrace of drone warfare in the war on terror.

So, we leave America with a new president in 2025, teetering between its three identities; its future direction sure to make an impact on the world outside. We hope that our study may be taken as a humble offering to remind Americans of this dimension of American identity.

It is important to recognize that even if Trump is not on the scene, Trumpism is far from over. It represents the beliefs, values, and ideas of American predator identity, which is rooted in culture and history and is, therefore, an essential part of what it means to be American. This is a reality that both national and international commentators cannot ignore but too frequently do. US history has also shown that backlashes from primordial and predator identities accompany gains made by pluralists, and the reality was that those identities were not going away. Trump and American leaders well into the future would have to navigate between all three identities.

It is appropriate here to return to the origin story of the USA as it provides us with a standard and a marker. It also reminds us of the wisdom of the Founding Fathers by providing the nation with the guiding principles for life, even in our times. The least they deserve is a salute. Remember that the only book George Washington wrote was called *Rules of Civility and Decent Behavior in Company and Conversation.* For Washington, true Americans were clearly civil, decent in their behavior, and respectful of each other. That maxim applies to every variety of American. This is particularly the case after an election has been decided. Otherwise, the democratic system the Founding Fathers devised, which has seen the nation hold a presidential election every four years like clockwork since the late eighteenth century, will not endure. Americans can do no better than to refer to the common sense and wisdom of the American Founding Fathers. In terms of the presidency, whoever is in the White House, the challenge for the incumbent is to bring their thinking in line with that of the broader vision of the Founding Fathers. The greater the distance between the individual and that vision, the more difficult the journey to it.

In the meantime, we prayed with humility and love in our hearts that Americans of all persuasions would join the battle to meet the challenges that lay ahead for Americans and larger humanity—the well-being of whom was also at the core of the Founding Fathers' universalist vision. We also prayed that the extraordinary experiment the United States provided to the world regarding the vision of the great Founding Fathers would continue to flourish. We were confident that the resolve, courage, and compassion engendered by that vision would stand America in good stead as it set about overcoming the challenges that awaited it in the coming time. This is precisely where America stood in 2025: America was at the crossroads.

Index